JOURNEY TOWARD
THE CRADLE OF MANKIND

GUIDO GOZZANO

Journey Toward the Cradle of Mankind

Translated by David Marinelli

THE MARLBORO PRESS | NORTHWESTERN
Evanston, Illinois

The Marlboro Press/Northwestern
Evanston, Illinois 60208-4210

Printed in the United States of America

ISBN 0-8101-6007-2 (cloth)
ISBN 0-8101-6008-0 (paper)

Library of Congress Cataloging-in-Publication Data

Gozzano, Guido, 1883–1916.
    [Verso la cuna del mondo. English]
    Journey toward the cradle of mankind / Guido Gozzano ; translated
by David Marinelli.
        p. cm.
    Translation of: Verso la cuna del mondo.
    "A poet's exploration of the myth and squalor of early twentieth-
century India."
    "First English-language publication."
    ISBN 0-8101-6007-2 (cloth : alk. paper).—ISBN 0-8101-6008-0
(pbk. : alk. paper)
    1. Gozzano, Guido, 1883–1916—Journeys—India. 2. India—
Description and travel. I. Marinelli, David. II. Title.
PQ4817.O9V4713 1996
858'.91203—dc20
    [B]   95-26730
                                                             CIP

The paper used in this publication meets the minimum requirements of the
American National Standard for Information Sciences—Permanence of
Paper for Printed Library Materials, ANSI Z39.48-1984.

Contents

Introduction

I

Guido Gozzano, one of the major twentieth-century Italian poets, led a short life poor in external events. He was born into a well-to-do Turin family, and spent most of his time either in the Piedmontese capital or in the family villas in Agliè Canavese. Although beginning in 1904 he studied law at the University of Turin, his interests were literary, and he began publishing poems when he was twenty. His first volume of verse, *La via del rifugio* [The Road to Shelter, 1907], made him known overnight. The travels that Gozzano began to undertake that same year with a view to easing his chest trouble culminated, in 1912, in a trip to India. His second and most important book of poems, *I colloqui* [The Colloquies, 1911], established him as one of Italy's leading poets. His last collection, *Le farfalle* [Butterflies], was published posthumously. Guido Gozzano, who had been born in 1883, died in 1916 of tuberculosis.

In Italian literary history Gozzano is usually classified with the *Crepuscolari,* a loose movement of young poets (Sergio Corazzini, Marino Moretti, and others) writing during the first two decades of this century. These "Twilight Poets" abandoned the heroic rhetorical abundance of Gabriele D'Annunzio in favor of quiet, provincial themes; they shunned verbal virtuosity in favor of the subdued expression of everyday situations and emotions.

Though Guido Gozzano shares a number of sources (the French, Flemish, and Belgian post-Symbolist poets, such as Jammes, Maeterlinck, Samain, and Verhaeren) with the *Crepuscolari* movement, his sense of form is more disciplined and he is more firmly rooted in reality.

It is no accident that Gozzano's best poems, "L'amica di nonna Speranza" [Grandma Hope's Friend], "Paolo e Virginia," and, most famous of all, "La signorina Felicita," are verse narratives. As the title of his finest book of verse, *The Colloquies,** suggests, the poet is interested in conversation, in dialogue. His subject matter is down to earth (middle-class women and provincial milieux such as they were in his day and had been for the generations immediately preceding his own), though his verbal tours de force and his irony manage to maintain a delicate equipoise between evocation and criticism. Gozzano's unique voice is a wonderful balancing act between sympathy for and gently ironic detachment from the characters he paints and their "good things in the worst of taste." The confrontation between threadbare reality and the exuberant, joyous use of language generates poetic fireworks.

This direct, amiable joining of involvement and ironic distance packaged in traditional verse forms results in a poetic voice which, while not profound, is invariably winning and enjoyable without being superficial. Not only does Gozzano lovingly recreate a bygone world peopled by sympathetic and often faintly ridiculous person-

---

*More properly translated as *The Conversations* or *The Talks*. The Italian is a common word while its English cognate is decidedly not.

ages, he also manages to yearn for them in a self-critical way that always keeps the reader guessing as to his real attitude. In "Miss Felicity" he would love to spend the rest of his days in the Canavese countryside with a simple, plain, and rather homely girl; he longs to leave the "futile" intellectual and material cares of Turin for the wholesome country life, but he cannot do so. He sees his dilemma from the outside as absurd and more than a bit foolish, yet he is unable to escape it: the longing for the honest simplicity of an earlier time is genuine but impossible, and he is constantly aware of it. Miraculously, the "splendid sentimental young romantic" of yesteryear and the ironic observer coexist, as equals.

For a poet largely unknown in English, Gozzano has attracted a fair amount of attention recently. There now exist two complete versions of *The Colloquies:* by Michael Palma (1981) and by J. G. Nichols (1987). Palma's translation for Princeton University Press, *The Man I Pretend to Be,* also includes a number of selected poems (and the Italian originals on the facing page) plus a substantial bibliography; in Nichols's volume (published by Carcanet) a number of letters complement the poems. Rhyme is the very stuff of Gozzano's poetry, setting in relief as it does the conflict between traditional form and subversive content; and both translators use it. Nichols's more playful and allusive approach is the more successful, though it is no easy matter to do justice to Gozzano in translation.

But the attempt has been made. The essential Gozzano, *The Colloquies,* is now available to readers of English. And although he is still far from widely known outside his own language, a basis now exists to broaden our acquaintance with an uncommonly appealing writer. All the more reason to introduce readers to his major prose work: *Verso la cuna del mondo*.

II

"Even in this enchanted place I feel homesick."

GOZZANO set out from Genoa for India in February 1912 with the ostensible purpose of treating the tuberculosis that would kill him a few years later. It was his first and only journey outside Europe, and he took along credentials from two newspapers, with the understanding that he was to write dispatches of what he saw. The poet-cum-exotic traveler turned out to be eminently unsuited for his journalistic mission. The trip lasted three months, of which some six weeks were spent on the subcontinent, almost entirely in Bombay and Ceylon.

Even a cursory glance at the titles of his "letters from India" reveals that their author could not possibly have visited most of the places he writes about.* The pieces Gozzano did in 1912 and 1913 were cribbed from at least half a dozen sources, chief among them Pierre Loti's *L'Inde (sans les anglais)* (1903) and Paolo Mentegazza's

---

*There is considerable disagreement as to what Gozzano actually saw in India. His letters to friends and family would seem to indicate that he did not leave Bombay except for a trip to Ceylon while other sources claim he traveled to Goa and Benares. In either case, the articles are essentially works of the imagination.

L'India (1884). Despite the wealth of facts, details, and situations he plundered from these popular contemporary travel books, Gozzano steers a middle course, avoiding the melancholy wonder and anti-British sentiment of the French novelist and the prosaic moralizing of the Italian physician Mentegazza. Here, as in his verse, Gozzano approaches his subject with a complex blend of realism, ironic distance, and lyric involvement.

Most of all, the contribution of Loti, Mentegazza, and the others is to furnish the poet with the standard Baedeker sights—descriptions of the Taj Mahal, Agra, Golconda, Benares, Goa, Jaipur, the Tower of Silence—that are the points of departure for his semifictional rambles, responses to the fin-de-siècle fascination with "ghost cities" (the European period equivalents are Venice, Bruges, and, to a lesser extent, Prague). Gozzano supplements these by describing the few places we are certain he did actually visit, Ceylon and Bombay, though there is no internal evidence in the individual pieces to distinguish experience from invention. The Piedmontese poet's ransacking of travel literature to reinforce the evocation of venues he visited in his imagination follows a method wholly in agreement with his approach to his sentimental journey across the subcontinent. In an undated letter from Kandy to Candida Bolognini he writes:

> I have looked at India with the eye of a poet. I haven't looked at it in depth; I enjoyed it on the surface. I didn't come here prepared the way scholars and archaeologists are. I know nothing about archaeology; I don't go deeply into things. I live on their beauty, I savor it, I make it my own, I seek to capture a bit of it in my letters, in my poems.

Thus he begins with familiar or (less familiar) personal Indian locales as raw material for poetic treatment.

Gozzano's perspective may be lyrical; his initial response is one of enthusiastic fascination. More than once the enchanted traveler declares that he never supposed he would find fabled India intact to this degree. He is "dumbfounded" and "cannot see his fill" of the pink city of Jaipur. The Taj Mahal compels his "admiration and total reverence." He is spellbound by the thespian art of a Devadasi, and by the alien Parsee funeral customs in "The Tower of Silence." Yet his admiration is not wholly uncritical, and his ironic sixth sense is alert to the gulf between himself and Indian culture; it is contemplating this abyss between sensibilities that leads him to observe that "the Westerner who returns to India no longer recognizes his cradle."

Gozzano's Indian pilgrimage, essentially, is an exploration of self. The writer's "twilight" perplexity and uneasiness in the dead cities of Goa and Golconda reveal at least as much about his persona as they do about the places described. Initially wonderfully exotic, Hindu temples soon inspire dread and revulsion before "savage idolatry." Nature, which the poet clung to in *The Colloquies* as the only force immune to his sneer, fails him now (as it also did in *Butterflies:* converts make bad poets). On Elephanta Island, for instance, he would like to venture off the beaten path, but "the refuge of the green night" is teeming with cobras: at its most inviting, tropical nature is "enchanting but frightening," fraught with danger.

Here as well, Gozzano's enthusiasm quickly gives way to anxiety: "It's a genuine Garden of Eden that excites even someone like me who finds it hard to become excited about anything," he writes to his sister Erina. Later in the trip he finds that "the plant life is too intense; it's suffocating." In Ceylon some "pathetic-looking European geraniums are stunned by the climate and chagrined by the surrounding flora"—flora he describes as "demented." Much like the geraniums he speaks of, Gozzano is intimidated by the "monstrous" lush nature enveloping him, cowed by the abundance of health that so contrasts with the slow death at work within him.

Still, somehow, he manages to retain his essential self, his sense of humor and irony, in the heart of deepest India: interspersed among his expressions of wonder, distress, and fear are evocations of his fellow European travelers. These vignettes of persons conspicuously out of place range from descriptions of amusing eccentrics abroad to tales of established expatriates and slightly faded demimondaines: a pompous, stamp-collecting German professor; Portuguese monks in Goa; a French consular agent who decimates his relatives and colleagues with frivolously homicidal vows to the goddess Tharata Ku Wha; proper Englishmen, Englishwomen, and an Italian doctor who accompany the author on a picnic at the Tower of Silence; and a pair of lively French courtesans working their way through the East. Though Gozzano seems fondest of the false *Parisiennes,* all of these characters share his enchanted exile, providing both paradoxical contrast to exotic sights and the solace of the familiar. On an illusory journey toward the cradle of mankind, the comforts of companionship sweeten the bitterness of impending decay and death: "It is better to mock the fatalism that weighs down upon men and the world by humming tunes from a comic opera."

David Marinelli

Translator's Note

My translation is based on Giorgio De Rienzo's edition of *Verso la cuna del mondo* (Milan: Mondadori, 1983). The textual differences between this and previous versions are minor. When Gozzano's book was first published (by Treves, in 1917), the pieces that constitute it were arranged chronologically according to what was thought to have been Gozzano's itinerary. For his part, De Rienzo places the articles in the sequence of their first appearance in print (in 1914 and 1915); the pieces that appeared after Gozzano's death he groups as an appendix. De Rienzo argues that the order of the "letters" and the datelines added in the 1917 edition were aimed at creating a unified book, which was probably not in keeping with the author's intentions.

Sound as this position may be for scholarly purposes, the average reader expects a certain degree of narrative coherence. I have therefore eliminated the (at best, misleading) date headings and arranged Gozzano's articles according to a more or less straightforward south-north progression; that is, I start in Ceylon and end in Jaipur.

I have left out three pieces as being alien to the book as a whole: they are "On the Fiery Ocean," a sentimental tale about the despairing love of a half-Indian woman for the narrator's best friend; "Rebellious India," a description of the caste system and of Indian Anglomania; and, its tragic pendant, "The Holocaust of Cawnpore." I have placed "Goa A Dourada" in the middle of the book because it is in many ways the text that is most central to the whole. And *Journey Toward the Cradle of Mankind* concludes not with "Fakirs and Charlatans" but with "Jaipur: The Pink City," because I find it more like Gozzano, "the man I never am, but feign to be," to take leave of India with "who knows how many pensive little faces and dangling tails" rather than with regretful effusions at having to bid adieu to the Taj Mahal.

JOURNEY TOWARD
THE CRADLE OF MANKIND

Christmas in Ceylon

Waking in this climate is such gentle agony. Numbed by the hothouse atmosphere, my mind takes some time to revive, struck by what feels like a rapid succession of camera flashes, as if in sleep my consciousness had fled to the remotest land of its yearnings only to be forced to return in a few seconds' time. Reason, however, awake and alert, goads the torment, inquiring, commenting, mocking: "'Tis futile to deceive me, o nocturnal wanderer! I am in Ceylon, I know I am in Ceylon! 'Tis futile to bring me a piece of Piedmontese landscape, the smile of a friend, or my mother's face with each awakening. I know I am dreaming. The faint ringing of bells you invent is quite a good imitation of my native country at Yuletide, but it isn't real. What is real is the deafening choir of parrots and apes on my bungalow roof. In a few seconds I shall wake up in Ceylon, in my solitary shelter, in the depths of a tropical rain forest."

I wake up. I am in Ceylon. My eyes are wide open. Through the white netting I see the furniture in my room. Patrick is standing, waiting with a pot of tea. I am wide awake; yet, through the forest, the faint sound of bells continues. I pull aside the mosquito bar and leap from my bed with a look of surprise so intense that the elderly Singhalese *boy* grows worried.

"What is the matter with you, master?"

"Nothing, my dear fellow. I feel fine, but whatever is that sound?"

"Christmas. It's the six o'clock service at the Kandy Mission."

Kandy, six hours off in the depths of the valley, can be heard all the way up here.

Patrick is a Christian. He wears his thin gray hair wound up in curls beneath a curved tortoiseshell comb, wears only a woman's red-and-blue checked skirt; on his bare chest, a scapular of celluloid and a small silver cross hang between amulets against poisons, cobras, and witchcraft; yet he is a Christian. He is a pure Aryan, with a noble Socratic face that very much reminds me of a frightfully distinguished instructor at the university—so much so that I still hesitate when I order him to prepare my bath or polish my boots.

"Christmas! Christmas! Don't you hear the bells?"

Matthew, the other *boy*, enters rejoicing, his brilliant white teeth gleaming in his bronzed face. Matthew is only twenty and speaks seven languages. He is a good hunter and excellent cook—no one can tenderize and fry the wood of the traveler palm or cook the meat of the scaly anteater or fruit bat better than he.

With these two companions and the bungalow care-taker—a staff barely adequate in this land where labor is divided according to age and caste—I have been living for almost a month in the last rest house which admirable British foresight has provided to the visitor. I wasted a good deal of time and money (too much money for an entomologist man of letters without adequate funding from his country's publishers and museums) in Colombo and Kandy amidst the gay enticements of the international hotels. I owe this blissful retreat to the good offices of the Dutch consul to Ceylon.

The rest house on Adam's Peak is tiny and modest, and I am not proud of the fact that the German crown prince spent the night here last year when he came to Ceylon for an elephant hunt. Alas, the dwelling is by no means imperial! It is as clean and drab as a railway station or a single-floor Japanese home, and it is surrounded by a white-columned porch, with the roof amply overhanging it—as is the case with all houses in the tropics—so you can close the window grating in the evening to protect yourself from unwelcome felines. In Europe, men put tigers in cages; here the tigers force men into cages. Not tigers actually, of which there are none in these forests, but the leopard and the Singhalese black panther, a much dreaded creature indeed. The indescribably melancholy rooms are laid out around a small courtyard or central patio consisting of whitewashed brickwork halfway up the wall; from there on up they are of openworked wood and, as such, open to the gentlest refreshing breeze. The tiniest winged creatures of the jungle, the Bengal thrushes, enter freely, with the astonishing trust the animals in India have for humans.

There is a bedroom as plain as a Carthusian monk's, a parlor of some European pretension, a kitchen, and a vast pantry, which I use as a laboratory and to store my crates and jars. In front of the house there is a small, ironic garden with a triangular flower bed, where the caretaker lovingly tends some pathetic-looking European geraniums stunned by the climate and chagrined by the surrounding flora. It is within this hermitage that the distant sounds of the Mission reach me this morning.

For the first time since I have been away from home I feel the faint pang of homesickness, barely perceptible but as gnawing and vexing as the earliest announcement of a toothache. I who had boasted of being immune to it! Alas, you can pretend to be Robinson Crusoe or a Buddhist monk, but you cannot break away from your essence, which is not only what it is but what it has been, and your psyche is helpless to dispel thousands and thousands of years of European evolution and twenty centuries of Christianity. Homesickness—the formidable, indescribable malady compounded of vague feelings much like fear and regret.

REVIVED by a bath, I walk outside to relax in the forest's awakening, a constant source of delight and wonder to my European eyes. I follow a barely perceptible path through the dense greenery, yet for the first time this delightful nature seems disturbing and hostile, like an antediluvian landscape in which a plesiosaur or iguanodon could appear at any moment. Through the tangle of demented foliage I hear once again, rising from the depths of the valley, the sound of the Mission bells. Then they stop; I have never felt so alone, though Patrick and Matthew are walking behind me carrying guns, nets, and tweezers. Still, we won't kill anything today—Gautama's brother, Francis of Assisi, was born in my country: Supreme Goodness incarnate, which comes to earth once every few millennia, has "arisen" once again in an "awakened one."

WE move along these narrow tracks resembling passageways through the greenery, dug out at night by wild elephants. It is 8:00 A.M., which means it is almost midnight in Italy. At this hour family and guests are surrounded by mistletoe and holly, and the windows are brightly lit in the icy darkness of a snow-covered Christmas Eve. Here it is a summer's morning—blinding light mitigated by the tree ferns that transform everything below into a green underwater shimmer—the never-ending hothouse warmth of the equatorial belt, a nameless fifth season I have dubbed Euphoria, the blissful madness that accompanies the interminable sufferings of consumptives. In this eternal warmth, eased at night or in the evening by an hour of torrential rain, plant life assumes incredible dimensions, lines, and colors. This beauty, coupled with the unchanging season, adds a further gnawing perplexity to my homesickness—a bewildering thought that the summers, autumns, and winters immortalized in masterpieces of European poetry, painting, and music are nothing more than the product of a given latitude; sadness at the relativity of all things, even those we worship as divine and immortal; still deeper sadness at the thought that this perpetually green earth is nothing more than a narrow zone of everlasting summer which, in the beginning, once covered the entire globe; a childish consternation that Italy is already plunged deep in the downward curve of earth's dying, that winter is the image that foretells the eternal Arctic night that will draw ever nearer with time, overtaking the last specimens of doomed humanity in this privileged tropical zone.

My Christmas is not a cheerful one and the flora on all sides provides no consolation. I am constantly reminded of the terrible distance from home. Not even by lowering one's eyes to the ground can the illusion be sustained—

my feet move through moss and monstrous lichens resembling polyps or masses of mother-of-pearl, then I tread on the ash-gray carpet of the blue Singhalese mimosa, my steps leaving a strange imprint that broadens almost instantly with the painful convulsion of an injured mollusk. On either side and above me is the joy of plant life and living fauna: strange insects (*fasmidæ, phillum,* etc.) imitate the branches and leaves; enormous butterflies enchant in flight like green and blue embers and, once at rest on a branch, close up into dead, gray leaves. Strange flowers, petals of rose- and blood-colored flesh, white or blue porcelain, flowers remote from our own, leaves fairer than flowers—heart-shaped, chalice-shaped, shield-shaped, lobed, serrated, fringed—white-veined with blue and red, red-veined with white and violet, tree ferns agile as green fountains, dwarf ferns, capillaries that float in the air as at the bottom of a fish tank. Everything is the same as when time began, a time before man and his sufferings.

Eleven o'clock. The sun is almost directly overhead. The fairy-tale landscape dissolves into the green distance in a series of mirages; trunks snake in the air, which vanishes, quivering, like a brook. I return to the bungalow. On the threshold, Matthew, who is walking in front of me, stops and cries loudly in frightened jubilation: "Cobra! Cobra! The best wish for you!"

What a strange imagination these Indians have, to symbolize joyful hope in a message of certain death! "Ckatura Tka" (Seven More Steps) the Singhalese call it, because it is said that the victim reels seven more steps, then falls to the ground, dead. It is surely one of the most lethal reptiles, though it certainly doesn't look frightening. The one that greets me in the garden is not much larger than a grass snake and would quickly flee if the *boy* did not jump about screaming, poking at it with his net. The cobra has coiled, its neck puffed up, swollen with anger, on the erect upper half of its body, and the little triangular head—ruby-red eyes, forked tongue darting—turns this way and that as the beast readies to defend itself.

But the man leaves it be, the reptile unwinds and disappears into the forest. Praise be to him as well this Christmas Day.

I AM sitting at the table, alone. The small living room creates a certain illusion of Europe, an illusion that makes me more rather than less homesick. The contrast between the tropical cleanliness, the whitewashed walls open-worked in their upper part, and the presumptuous old heaviness of the sparse furnishings, which reminds me of a doctor's waiting room, is truly enormous: four rattan chairs, a divan giving up its straw ghost from myriad wounds, a console table in *style Empire,* upon it a Robert pendulum clock of some value, a bookshelf containing a huge Bible, on the walls a modern oleograph of the British royal family and two old etchings of seventeenth-century Amsterdam. These objects were taken from some old bungalow and brought to Ceylon during the period of Dutch rule, when Flemish traders sailed to the fabled island whose location was not clearly indicated on the maps, after an adventurous year aboard creaky vessels circumnavigating Africa and India.

Patrick and Matthew come and go silently, watching

my every gesture with the marvelous zealous devotion of Indian servants that surprises every traveler. On the center of the table, behind a tin, Matthew has placed a great bouquet of orchids, picked this morning in the jungle, and a plate of huge mangoes. I have grown accustomed to this strange fruit, which when you split it open offers a cool pulp, whipped like a sorbet, smelling of musk and creosote, that one would swear had been prepared by a confectioner, perfumer, or pharmacist. And you would swear a goldsmith had designed the orchids in front of me: petals of multicolored lacquer, quartz-powdered, fantastic, and sneering necks of Japanese dragons, petals that are gibbous, horned, curved, iridescent on the inside like the open thoraxes of slaughtered animals. The bunch of flowers is a plague nightmare come true, and in the sultry afternoon heat it exudes an unbearably fetid smell. I have this fabulous bouquet removed, which at this hour, in a European salon, would be a gift fit for a princess. I would be more than happy to trade it for a sprig of Christmas holly with red berries or a cluster of pearly mistletoe.

IT is the sultry afternoon hour, the hour of the tropical siesta on the deck chair, the hour of the silence propitious to the visit of the Bengal thrushes.

A flock of tiny thrushes, red or greenish speckled with white, storm from a wall of the living room—they explore it, fly through it, and return. They are alarmed when I abruptly reach out to pick up a book, swarm into the kitchen, return frightened by the bustle of the *boys,* whirl twice through the dining room, and take up positions in the openwork of the wall, waiting. Some of the more daring among them, judging that I have not decid-ed to leave, fly down, settle on the backs of the chairs, on the bookcases, on the floor, to peck at the lunch crumbs, and then, one by one, all fly down, hop about chirping softly, by now trusting the man in white. I toss a newspa-per to see how far their daring extends, and the reckless birds barely get out of the way.

In the silent, suffocating midday heat the arrogant chirping harmonizes with the ticktock of the old Robert that has marked the hours of so many exiled lives, har-monizes with the muted singing of the *boys*.

Patrick and Matthew have stopped bustling about. They are lying on the floor with their backs to the wall, sleeping and singing. Their indolent dream flows through their closed mouths as bizarre, somnolent music: action reflected, commentary on reality, para-phrase of solitude and exile, heat and silence.

From Ceylon to Madura

THIS dazzling island, too, fades into memory. Everyone is on deck to bid it farewell: London tourists who get as far as Colombo during their two-month race around the subcontinent, Dutch and Belgian cinnamon and pearl traders, Tamils returning to India after their annual stint on the Singhalese tea and coffee plantations—everyone is on deck, eyes fixed on the verdant land, each with different regrets. The ship leaves the port, pitching at the first fury of the open sea.

Suddenly, the island becomes blurred, as if to put an abrupt end to the melancholy farewells. In a few seconds, everything, from Adam's Peak to the coastal forests, is engulfed in a curtain of billowing clouds, dark and solid as if carved from bluish marble, while the sky around us remains azure and calm. In the dark frame, as in the oval of artificial clouds in paintings depicting Hell and deluges, blue, violent thunderbolts crisscross and explode; the scenery around us bathes in bright red flashes, outlining the disheveled palms in black. In the distance a torrential downpour, inconceivable in our latitudes, streaks the center of the scene with oblique stripes of glass. An indescribable rumbling as from an orchestra of a thousand mighty gongs accompanies the equatorial hurricane.

The ship sets out in calm waters, but in the offing the

sea is restless. The waves tremble continuously in the Gulf of Mannar, which, fortunately, we will cross in a single night. Before dawn tomorrow we shall land in Tuticorin, the southernmost city of Hindustan.

IT is dawn, but we have yet to sight land. The sea is still raging.

Luckily immune to seasickness, but numbed by a sleepless night and aching from the safety belts, I am lying in my cabin listening to the groanings of my neighbors, the clipped orders of the officers, and the booming of the ship's propeller, which at times races above water. It also stops turning; the boat comes to a halt. Staggering, I climb up on deck. The *Bangalore* "ha stoppato," an officer of the British India Company who insists on speaking Italian explains, "to wait for a tug. Around us lies an archipelago rich in pearls; we are among treacherous banks known only to the native fishermen."

This sea yields the most beautiful pearls in the world. I thought it would be different, rich in lights and vivid colors under a bright red sky. Instead it looks like a northern sea—indeed, a primordial ocean in which there is no clear separation between the waters and the continents. The horizon resembles molten lead, stirred not by the wind but by the current which surges and recedes in the shallow water. Here and there it foams and seethes as if tossed by the mass of a colossal underwater monster. The oppressive, dark sky, from which the sun projects its uneven beams, intensifies the illusion of an antediluvian ocean. I live in palpable fear of a huge back emerging, the high coiled neck and small voracious head of an icthyosaur. Bordered by foam, the small islands that link

Ceylon to the southern part of Hindustan gleam white on the horizon—islands so uniform and close together that, at low tide, they are used by elephants to migrate to the continent. For the Hindus they form the Bridge of Rama, the bridge used by the Vedic hero to assault the island of a captive Indian princess; for the Christians they are Adam's Bridge, trod by the first man when he was expelled from Eden with his mate.

The ship, at anchor in these surging, swelling waters, bobs and pitches restlessly.

The tug is nowhere in sight.

We got ashore at Tuticorin aboard a sort of steam barge, which they tossed us onto one by one, like bales of goods, waiting for the moment when the swells lifted the boat almost level with the steamship's cargo deck.

Tuticorin is the famous pearl city. Yet three years ago the English forbade pearl fishing here because the pearl banks were being mercilessly and unmethodically depleted. Cast aside in the deluded hope of finding the white treasures, discarded oyster shells form shoals fifteen to twenty meters high, creating new shorelines that have modified the coast over the centuries.

There are, of course, no pearls to be seen in the city of pearls. Those shown to us by the street sellers—too large and perfect, too white against their bronze-hued palms—look as if they had been manufactured by a German glass company in Bombay or Calcutta. Those sold by licensed jewelers, who hold permits and provide consular guarantees, are astronomically expensive and not at all beautiful. The best merchandise is withheld from the traveler, intercepted for the large markets in London and Amsterdam.

I cannot leave out the carvers' quarter. The incredibly refined skill these artisans possess in the working of ebony, ivory, and mother-of-pearl is handed down within their caste. They carve and sculpt elephants, amulets, and small idols according to models unchanged over the centuries. A blind man had carved the entire legend of Rama from an elephant's tusk, and the episodes unfolded in a spiral of groups not without a certain liveliness and grace, with an art similar to that of our primitives.

We leave Tuticorin for Madura. Once again we board one of the indefinably exotic Indian railway trains: large, virtually square cars with peaked roofs in which English refinement contrasts with the exotic, immense, fanlike *panka* (the native counterpart to the electric fan, also in use); the signs and advertisements in English, Tamil, Arabic, and Singhalese; the strange flowers on the dining-car tables; the exotic servants wearing white shirts, barefoot and silent yet grand as sultans. We are traveling to Madura, the "Heart of Brahma," the native name for this part of southern Hindustan formed by the three states of Travancore, Madura, and Taniore, where Brahmanism remains untouched, immune to Islam, which has spread to northern and central India, and to Buddhism, which dominates the island of Ceylon. I immediately recognize the city of Madura from afar, thanks to the familiar silhouette of its truncated pyramids rising above the green of the palms. I had imagined the tall *gopuram* of Brahma to be of pure gold; instead they are bright red, and the gold does not become evident until you are nearer, alternating with blue and green to accentuate the figures covering their immense surfaces. By the time we reach the station it is too late to visit the temple.

The day is drawing to a close—the sky turns red for an instant and the stars appear one by one, as on a stage when the house lights are suddenly turned off.

IN the land of Brahma we are the guests of the Belgian Missions of the Unshod Carmelites, thanks to a letter of introduction from the bishop of Bombay. There are no hotels in Madura; the one at the railway station (with a mostly native service, the screeching and rumbling of the trains, and the din of pilgrims) is out of the question.

Instead I awake in this neat, clean room with its view of a peaceful garden. This is no longer the wild flora of Ceylon. In these flower beds Bengal roses and European vegetables grow side by side, and such is the effect that, this January morning, I have the illusion of walking in a Piedmontese garden on one of our fairest summer days. Then a swarm of green parrots and an overly large, brilliant, decidedly un-European butterfly remind me that I am in the tropics, almost assaulting me with the nightmare of eternal summer. From far away the steady, discordant sound of tam-tams, gongs, and whistles drowns out the ringing of the Catholic bells—a savage orchestra that speaks to me of fearful mysteries and idolatry.

"Idolatry!" says the missionary accompanying me, a young Fleming hardened to all the trials and tribulations of the region. "Idolatry is the relentless scourge of these people. They are unacquainted with their own sacred literature, which contains masterpieces of edifying philosophy, excellent preparation for receiving the light of Christianity, as are their own priests, who specialize in superficial, absurd practices passed down by the castes. The Hindus need idols. We are forced to reveal Christian symbols in the most concrete form—the image. Everything pertaining to the Gospel, moral discipline, everything abstract, has no effect on these spirits used to a Dravidian Olympus populated by thousands of gods. They are docile souls eager to believe, but a heretical faith makes them pair the Trinity of Brahma with the Trinity of Christ, Maya Devi with the Virgin Mary, Mara with Satan. For them Satan is not Evil, but a terrible power, almost respectable, certainly due higher regard than the Divinity, to be placated with gifts and garlands. They accept Christ, the priests accept him, though to place him as an avatar, another incarnation, between Ganesa and Parvati. It would probably be easier to enlighten a Niam Niam than these minds clouded by an idolatry three millennia old."

We enter the crowded church. The mass is coming to an end: the devout are genuflected almost on all fours with an absorption virtually unheard of in Europe. Then I notice that the naves are divided into three walled-off sections: without these divisions none of the faithful would attend, because even the most convincing exposition of the Gospel would never induce an Indian to come close to an Indian of another caste.

The missionary draws my attention to strange amulets on the bronzed necks of the kneeling faithful: tiger fangs and phallic lingam alongside scapulars, small crosses, and medallions of the saints.

I SET out across the city upon an avenue lined by colossal banyans whose trunks and roots form a tunnel. At intervals among the roots there are small temples, remotely archaic tabernacles containing tiny, horrid, grotesque idols like fetuses sculpted in stone; and they are contained by stout gratings as if they were ferocious beasts. Along with the small temples I notice high-backed granite chairs set up for women carrying burdens, so they can set down their enormous amphorae and heavy bundles and pick them up again unaided. Men walk by, dark Tamils, an aboriginal race of low caste, and light-skinned Brahmins, who shun clothing and adornment but are dignified in their complete nudity with no ornament except the holy waistcord, baptismal symbol of high caste, and the same monogram of Vishnu I see painted upon the houses, the trunks of trees, and the broad brows of the elephants.

Madura is the holy city of Brahmanism, the goal of endless pilgrimages, site of constant adoration, where life and reality serve no purpose other than contemplation and prayer. The city contains more temples than houses, more priests than burghers. The great temple of Shiva and Meenakshi, "the fish-eyed goddess," is a city within a city and a labyrinth. Like all Brahmin temples, it consists not of a single building but of various structures enclosed by concentric courtyards, in ever larger enclosures, each enclosure crowned by two *gopuram* with cusps whose absurd symbolism soars eighty meters into the air. The dwellings of the upper-caste Brahmins located in the courtyards, the pools for the ablutions of the faithful, statues, huge idols, covered markets—everything contributes to the material and moral life of a people in worship.

I arrive at the temple, almost unaware of the fact, along a wide road lined by verandaed houses that would remind one of provincial Rome if the columns were classical rather than square Indian ones with their elephant-head capitals and grinning monsters. The road leads to the first pyramid, continues inside the pyramid, and the secular city continues inside the holy city. I walk from the blinding light into the religious semidarkness. I lean against the granite wall in order to get my bearings and feel the granite palpitate, give way: it is one of the holy elephants, a decrepit colossus that seems to be carved into the temple stone itself. Its proboscis brushes against my hands and face with an indulgent caress; another one is stretched out and shows its immense curved back in profile, blocking at least half the road, forcing the traffic and bustle of the faithful to detour. Three tiny newborn elephants trot by with a tinkling of bells; a zebu cow approaches gingerly, sniffing at the greens and fruits offered by the faithful: cows and elephants of this enclo-sure are sacred animals destined for religious processions, living idols in Madura Temple. Even their excrement is revered. Over the entire temple hangs a cloud of idolatry that makes me think of the fetishism of darkest Africa, not the religious speculations of the Vedas. The proces-sion of Parvati passes by, a ritual repeated twice daily, car-rying the images of the wife of Shiva, visiting all the tabernacles of the holy enclosure. The fetish, a doll of solid gold with a thin waist, full breasts, and round eyes of inlaid onyx beneath a high, jewel-encrusted miter, appears and disappears behind the drapes of the rich sedan chair. The scene is accompanied by a rumble of tam-tams, a discordant blare of trumpets and whistles, inspiring in the foreigner a sense of fearful distrust and repugnance, like a gloomy, grotesque mystery. The tem-ple abounds in treasures and the grossest neglect.

I venture into the second, then the third enclosure, walk from the shade into the penumbra, enter again beneath the immense sepulchral vaults constructed of monolithic blocks fifteen meters long, placed together to form a titanic roof that brings Ancient Egypt to mind. Beneath the central *gopuram* the columns multiply, are lost in the shade like the centuries-old trunks in a beech forest. Outside the sun is still beating down. Here, however, it is darkest night studded with an infinity of votive lamps that outline, without illuminating, the columns, holy railings, and huge idols. My eyes gradually begin to make out the throng of flesh, metal, and stone.

I did not honestly think I would find fabled India this intact, the shapes I had known from woodcuts and books ever since I was a child. I am disappointed, however, in my philosophical expectations, in my love for the greatest religion that has ever expressed our human anguish at being born, at having to die.

Is this the land of Brahma? Of Brahma "the Ineffable, of him we are not permitted to name if we wish him to appear"? Where the divine name is a filthy fetishism practiced by a mad people that has reduced abstract speculation to absurd symbolism; a people that adores these symbols and ignores them, a people that genuflects, cries, invokes, and knows not what, knows not why?

I continue walking in the semidarkness, still between the endless columns, underneath the flat vaults, and am guided by two natives carrying resinous torches. The walls catch a faint light, and strange divinities appear, again enclosed like well-kept beasts in cages with sturdy bars. Ganesa, the God of Wisdom, appears most often. He is depicted with all his kin, sporting an elephant's head or as a nameless divinity with a cow's body and a female head; the bovine, gibbous body is faithfully copied from the model of the native zebu, the female face is modeled on the Indian type, with jewels on her forehead, ears, and nose, and the excruciating smile of a convulsive *bayadère*. The torches held above our heads disturb the sleep of the great vampire bats, and our faces are fanned by the flapping of their silent wings, which resemble broad strips of black silk.

We walk out into the open, into the central courtyard. In the light of sunset appears the great temple pool—a hundred meters long, rectangular, enclosed on all sides by marble staircases surrounded by graceful columns, which evoke the elegance of a Pompeian peristyle. After the gloomy darkness, yellow torches, and fearsome idols, the soul is refreshed on the shore of this crystal-clear water; smooth as a mirror, its terse clarity reflects the sky, the bright red-and-blue clouds, and the first stars of oncoming night. The *gopuram* dominating Madura extend their cusps on all sides, far and near. Before the sun sets I want to climb the sides of the entrance *gopuram,* to see the famous sculptures close up and feel them. Every available bit of space here is carved with high-relief divinities and monsters so bold they seem to gesticulate, work themselves free, fall toward the infidel and rend him to pieces with their twenty scimitar-wielding arms; their cohorts of tigers and serpents ascend to the summit where the cusp challenges the sky with twenty spears of various lengths. It is all a symbolic theogony, a person-ification of the forces of Nature which the Hinduist mind has divided and subdivided with a tragic, grotesque, analytical spirit, exciting fear and a smile. From the side of this *gopuram* one has a panoramic view of the city and the surrounding countryside, where other pagodas rise and fall above the waves of the bright-green coconut palms. Many of these pagodas are Christian churches, for Saint Thomas preached Christianity in this part of India. In the course of the centuries mission followed mission, unmolested, well-received by the priests themselves in this land that tolerates every form of worship so long as you adore, so long as you believe.

So the name of Christ was uttered here while Europe was still pagan. This thought engenders a highly exotic perplexity, one of mysterious distance in space and time. The thought seems irreconcilable with this pyramid populated by heroes and monsters, which provides a stairway to the sky of flame. In the reddening heavens phalanxes of crows and parrots swirl and eddy, returning to their nests suspended between the sculptures of this frenzied Olympus. For the screeching of the feathered creatures, which comes from on high, harmonizes with the orchestral screeching issuing from the depths of the Temple, from all the temples near and far: rumbling tam-tams and strident whistles that speak of savage fury and idolatry.

A Vow to the Goddess Tharata Ku Wha

M Y baggage! My baggage!"

Lost! My new zinc chests, on which I had painted the Italian flag to make them stand out in the chaos of the train stations and docks—lost! Lost the tiger, panther, and python skins, the mortal remains of birds of prey: eight hundred birds of paradise from New Guinea, worth a fortune! The cases and jars of rare insects, all my spoils from a year of toil in exile—lost!

Lambahadam Station, buried beneath the green of the coconut palms at the very tip of southern India. I thought I was going to lose my mind. Add this to having to express oneself, haggle, and rave—in a language not one's own—with a native stationmaster, a bronzed Christ in braided livery. He tried to calm me by citing a case of priceless baggage being lost in the crisscrossed tangle of telegraph lines that encloses the entire peninsula like a net—a peninsula thirty times larger than Italy.

"I was a fool to try to cross Hindustan by train. This very moment I could be sailing on the calm blue Indian Ocean, reclining in a deck chair with a cigarette between my lips, the latest popular satire in my hands, waiting for the lunch bell to ring. My chests would be slumbering safe and sound in the depths of the hold. Damn it all!"

My traveling companion, a French consular agent I had met in Madura, has ceased consoling me with his mechanical "C'est rigolo, c'est rigolo." But look, here's the *boy* sent to the post office for the latest cables coming our way; he is bringing the mail, letters and periodicals forwarded from twenty stations: unpleasant news from Italy, a letter from my mother worried about a bullying old great-uncle—a Genoese priest, the tyrant and curse of the entire family since time immemorial—and three issues of one of the best Italian literary reviews. I open the first. Here is an article by Tito Vinadio, the most malignant name I know, followed by twenty pages on my latest book, which I had written with all the love of my youth and at the sacrifice of six years thereof. The article is sure to contain unflattering things about me. But no, it can't be! It isn't a review, but a series of amusing jibes, witticisms, and personal attacks, in the style of a drunken public scribe corrected by a peevish spinster schoolmarm. In the foremost magazine, the official voice of Italian literature! At home this sort of jest causes five minutes of bad temper and nothing more. But here, at the very tip of idolatrous India, in the refreshment room of a barbaric railway station, with my spirits already broken by mortal dread, the low blow produces disgust and unjust rancor toward my native land.

I spring to my feet. Oddly enough, I am no longer hurt; the anxiety and hatred have canceled each other out, suddenly erasing all pain.

"How much time do we have for a visit to the temples of Lambahadam? Excellent! Let's be off!"

OUTSIDE, three kinds of conveyance await us: cabs drawn by zebus, the humpbacked Indian bulls, with long, twisted, backward-bent horns painted in red and blue circles;

rickshaws, the little lacquer and bamboo cabs, drawn at great speed by naked natives; and elephants with high turrets for eight passengers—one hundred-year-old elephants, wrinkled as leather bags—their old hides also painted in bright colors and caparisoned in silk, in worn-out, faded velvets. There is not a single European to be seen: the surrounding crowd is composed entirely of natives—bronzed nudity, flashing white teeth, eyes too large to begin with made darker and larger still by kohl, with an art unknown to our most sophisticated society women; lively adolescent girls wearing nothing more than a slender chain around their waists, and a metal heart that moves back and forth insecurely over the spot it is meant to cover.

The town, all white or pink single-story houses, is neat and cheerful, hidden behind the shimmering green coconut and banana trees. The roofs are surmounted by long lines of crows, green lines of parrots, by endless tails of monkeys meeting for their morning confabulation. Our cavalcade places us at the height of the windows, and we see a woman inside combing her hair, a mother screaming at her child, a merchant counting his money, a statue of Vishnu, a statuette of twenty-armed Shiva, of elephant-headed Ganesa. From the window, men, women, and children smile and bow with their joined palms raised to the forehead in the Indian greeting.

"My baggage! My baggage!"

My drowsy mind, temporarily distracted by the odd spectacle, awakens with a painful start.

The turret is full: we two Europeans and a number of natives, also pilgrims to the Temple of the Cloud.

We arrive.

All is forgotten. Above the rolling sea of coconut palms, against the turquoise sky, the massive structure, made entirely of gold, rises: terraces, spires, cusps, domes, staircases piled one top of the other in a Babelic heap that surpasses and confounds every principle of architectural line and proportion; it is perhaps three times higher than the Great Pyramid and cannot be the work of man.

It is not the work of man, but a boulder that fell from the sky onto the endless Indo-Gangetic Plain, a geological oddity resulting from a primeval cataclysm. Once Vishnu had created the earth, he took what was left over, rolled it up into a ball, and cast it haphazardly into the void; when it fell upon the Lambahadam plain, it formed the four hundred-meter block that dominates the sea of green. Over the millennia men have worked it as one carves an elephant tusk; the living cliff is honeycombed with tunnels, verandas, stairways, and huge sanctuaries consecrated to the three thousand gods of Brahmin mythology. Sacred flames have burned there since time immemorial, and everything is covered, plated, with pure gold, for the faithful flock from all over India generously to offer coins and jewels.

We climb stairways that lead almost straight up, zigzags carved into the vertical walls; below us is the endless green plain, bound only by the sky-blue circle of the horizon, broken here and there by other cusps, the other domes of lesser temples. On every side there is a tumult of crows and holy vultures—a deafening, hostile shrieking. From the interior of each sanctuary rises a primitive singing of hymns, a raucous tam-tam, music that at times becomes as ferocious as a hundred roars, at times fades away to the buzz of a dying dragonfly.

"My baggage. My baggage."

We continue to climb. We cross more verandas, more corridors. Brahmins of lofty stature, naked except for a patch around their loins but nobler and grander than gentlemen dressed in shirt fronts, meet us, follow us with an absent gaze. All of them have the red trident of Vishnu painted on their foreheads, the same symbol that emblazons the lintels above entranceways, the trunks of palm trees, the heads of elephants and zebus. Walking from the blinding light into the deep sanctuaries, I am left in utter darkness for several seconds before I can make out the votive lamps, the blazing pyres before the godhead, the glittering of gold and gems on the multiple arms, the tiaras, the monstrous breasts, the elephantine trumpets. Columns, monolithic arches carved like point lace, hang numberless in the darkness, and I can hear a continuous chirping from the dark vaults, a silent fluttering of strips of black material—the vampire bats, bats as broad as an extended human arm, which by day hang by the thousands from the murky vaults and at night raid the fruit plantations.

We rest for perhaps an hour in the last sanctuary, at the pinnacle of the temple, seated in the cool semidarkness, as the sun outside is high and merciless. My eyes have grown accustomed to the dark. I look about the crypts of the godhead: each idol is enclosed in an iron cage like a dangerous feline, and the brazier that burns before it, with its bloody, flickering reflection, almost brings the frightening faces of the monster to life.

"My baggage. My baggage."

A Hindu policeman, who has heard my groans and seen me holding my head between my hands, approaches and asks us solicitously, "Have you suffered an injustice?"

"No, no injustice." My Parisian friend tells him why I am distressed. While they are talking, a Brahmin, a naked old man with a large white beard, gets up, turns to the policeman, who is looking at us, and smiles: "Gentlemen, the High Priest of Aparapandra, of the Goddess of Things Faraway, suggests a vow for your luggage. It costs very little, one rupee, and the result is guaranteed!" The policeman leaves, laughing.

A vow to the Goddess of Things Faraway? Of course! Where is this woman? That one over there? I offer her a penny and bow to the horrid, sinister-looking mug enclosed in one of the millennia-old cages. There are other priests standing around us in the dark, curious about the pair of *unclean ones* who are showing reverence to their godhead. One by one they come forward, offer their thanks to us: a vow to the God against Cobra Venom? To the God against Mishaps of the Journey? To the Goddess of Fecundity? To the God against the Evil Eye? To the Goddess Tharata Ku Wha: the Goddess of the Vanished Enemy?

What has the rabble done to the divine treasure of the Vedas? To what filthy idolatry has the sublime heritage of the Upanishads, essence of the Ineffable, the One, the Absolute, been reduced? A disgusting marketplace where every favor has its own charlatan, like a European department store where specializing salesmen sell each type of merchandise.

"The Goddess of the Vanished Enemy? What does that mean?"

"Death," the priest replies calmly, "or the suppression of whoever troubles you."

The image of Tito Vinadio flashes into my mind, sneering between his fair sideburns à la Camillo Cavour.

I say nothing, but my Parisian friend cries out enthusiastically: "Mais très bien ça! I, too, have at least twenty people I have no desire to see when I return to France!"

We approach another altar, laughing loudly. The priest, more decrepit and sinister-looking than the first, cuts a rectangle from a large palm leaf, hands it to me with a wet brush, nodding to me to write. I write the name "Tito Vinadio" and throw it onto the embers, which devour it with a crackling. The bony hand promptly tenders me another sheet. Another victim? I do not have any enemies. Whom else shall I eliminate? Ah, yes! Don Fulgenzi, the torment of our home. I write the name; the flames devour it. From the bony hand I receive another sheet; I search among my antipathies. Ah, yes, that detestable man with the hooked nose— unquestionably a jinx, because every time I ran into him everything went wrong; and I saw him often, on the streetcars, on the train, at the theater. I write, "Detestable anonymous man with the hooked nose."

A fourth sheet. No, no! That's enough! I laugh. But the jest has begun to make me shiver from fear, in the darkness, among these sinister idols, amidst the screeching of the vampire bats.

My Parisian friend is implacable. He writes sheet after sheet and throws them into the flames, entrusting all his relatives to the goddess' baleful offices.

"Ma tante Véronique! Mon oncle Alexis! Mon cousin Frédéric! Mon ami Chautel!"

I grab him by the shoulder and drag him off into the open, into sunlight. We descend the stairs, laughing.

"Combien en avez-vous foutu?"

"Three."

"*Seulement?* I rid myself of fourteen relatives and colleagues in the diplomatic corps!"

That evening—the train is already quite far from Lambahadam—my friend is hunched over the corner of a table in the dining car, writing a list of names and figures on the back of the menu. He stops speaking under his breath and lets out a laugh.

"Sorry, I'm finished now. I've made a list of those I exterminated. Not calculating the moral and material advantages to me of the disappearance of five colleagues, I should have an inheritance of 4,700,000 francs when I get back to France, if the Goddess Tharata Ku Wha has heard my prayers."

That night, no longer distracted by the landscape and the jest, I was seized again by distress over my lost treasures. Until dawn, I was tormented by insomnia and despair to the dizzying rhythm of the train. I had been asleep for perhaps an hour when I awoke to the joyful cries of my companion. We had arrived at the station in Kathalla.

"Mon ami! Come down! Quick!"

I sprang off the train. Ten paces from me, beneath the flowered veranda, were my new chests with their tricolors, piled in a neat pyramid, gleaming in the tropical sun.

First I touched them, then I embraced the embarrassed stationmaster, embraced an old Hindu woman who blanched with fear and fled, touching her amulets, embraced my companion, who was more frantic than myself, and we began to whirl around, holding hands, drawing little by little closer to one another until our bodies formed a whirling skein-winder.

"Long live France!"

"Vive l'Italie!"

The stationmaster separated us, calmed us down, and gently forced us to board the train again. I refused to get back on without a guarantee of advance telegraphic notice for my baggage all the way down the line to Bombay.

In the company of the unfailingly gay Parisian, the entire twenty-day trip was pure delight.

In Bombay, however—we had to part ways that day and embark on different steamers for our respective countries—I saw him suddenly turn pale as he held a letter between trembling fingers.

"Ah! Les malheureux!"

"What is it?"

"Mes cousins . . . "

"Well, what about them?"

" . . . crashed in a monoplane—dead. My uncle . . . gone hopelessly . . . mad."

I turned pale. I heard the three names again, again saw the dark cave of the vampire bats and the Brahmin with the white-haired chest and the goddess grinning from behind bars while the brazier sizzled away.

I comforted my friend, accompanied him to his ship, which weighed anchor that afternoon. A bit later I embarked for Italy with all my belongings. I was content. But ten days later, in Aden, I was handed a letter from my mother that sent a chill down my spine:

"I ought to have sent you this on black-bordered

paper, but that would be hypocritical. Don Fulgenzi departed from the living three days ago."

I was shaking. No. No! Is this a goddess, temple, witchcraft? I do not believe it! Two rash boys fall a thousand meters, the father goes insane, a nasty old man ceases to make life miserable for others. Isn't that all perfectly normal? Are you trembling? Are you too going mad, or theosophical? The dinner bell rang. The light, the flowers, the cut glassware, the lovely bare shoulders, and the good cheer of the officers brought me back to reality. Eight days later, landing at Genoa, I had forgotten everything.

MONTHS passed.

IN Venice the following autumn, I was sitting on a divan in the Viennese Salon, partly to take a rest, partly to enjoy from a distance, my eyes half closed, Krawetz's portrait of the fair siren.

My enjoyment was considerably diminished by two visitors examining the canvas from very near on: the one, tall and dark-haired, was supporting the other, who was small, stooped, a little old man with fairish hair on the nape of his neck. The dark-haired man turned. I recognized him. I went over and greeted him effusively. It was the painter Claudio Girelli. I looked at the old man. He wasn't old, but ill.

"You know our dear old Tito Vinadio, don't you?"

The ailing man drew his left hand from beneath the other's arm.

"Can't give you . . . eh, my right hand . . . any other way—"

Laughing and crying, he pulled his right hand from his pocket with his left and offered it to me inert, dangling like something not his own. He laughed and cried. Yet only half of his face moved, or rather, it twisted into an asymmetrical rictus that made me think of an ancient mask.

"Dear Girelli," he continued with a tearful smile, "is taking me along to the exposition, takes me along to the electrotherapeutic cl . . . cl . . . clinic."

" . . . electrotherapeutic clinic run by Professor Gaudenzi," the other finished, "who will cure our dear Vinadio in a few days' time. It's late. We have to go."

Mercifully, Girelli lifted the limp arm, placed it back in its pocket, and guided Vinadio away, one hand supporting him under the armpit. Before leaving, Girelli shot a glance at me. I had already resumed my place on the divan without a word.

"Don't waste your time at these foolish salons. . . . You must still be exhausted from your trip. You look a bit pale, too."

Am I going mad?

No, not yet. Perhaps I shall go mad the day I learn of the death of my third victim, the *detestable man with the hooked nose*. I haven't seen him again. Though for some time now a terrible thing has been happening. On the streetcar, in the theater, I have recognized a gentleman who used to keep the anonymous man company. I am barely able to resist the temptation to introduce myself to him, in order to ask him, as custom expects, what has become of his friend so-and-so.

If the other were then to answer, "Why, haven't you heard? You didn't know he died a year ago?" I, a threefold murderer, would jump off the streetcar or out of the theater and burst into the nearest police station to find shelter from my remorse in the punishing hand of human justice.

Yet I am certain that after having heard my breathless confession, the good judge, considering that human codes of law have yet to make provision for homicide by means of vows made to the Goddess Tharata Ku Wha, would console me with fatherly assurance; then, having nodded to two kindly bailiffs, would have me transferred not to prison but to a home for the mentally ill.

The Tower of Silence

Tʜɪs is not the title of a volume of Decadent verse.

The Tower of Silence is an excursion every Cook's *boy* in Bombay recommends to the traveler unsure of which sights to visit. The Tower of Silence—actually, the Towers, for there are five *Dakmas* where the Parsees expose the bodies of their dead to the vultures. I thought they were made up by some writer of adventure novels, the kind we love when we are young, in which a young explorer, seduced by the languorous eyes of a maharaja's daughter, drugged and rolled up in a sheet and about to be exposed to the vultures, and saved at the last minute by a faithful servant, is united in holy matrimony with her paramour.

The Towers actually exist, and are still as they were a thousand years ago. Everything is unchanged in British India, everything is the way it is presented in books and oleographs: dancing *bayadères,* colossal temples, and nimble fakirs. Woe betide those who feel repugnance for the commonplace or a longing for the unheard-of—here a writer is in constant danger of experiencing acute regret, the indefinable irritation of life imitating literature. There is no means of escape except to leave your hotel sans guide and friends and to lose yourself in the vast, luminous metropolis with its ogee-shaped build-

45

ings, terraces, verandas, and stairways, crowned with flowers and palm trees—buildings in the English Gothic style embellished by the demands of the climate, immune to the foul art nouveau that poisons the great cities of Europe; buildings that look like Sleeping Beauty's castle and are in fact the Municipal Corporation Building, the General Post Office, etc. You then discover the unusual in small, everyday things: the sepoy, with blue eye makeup extending to his temples to protect him from the evil eye of strangers, who stands at attention when you ask for directions; the chauffeur who wears the trident of Vishnu beneath his bright red celluloid visor; a streetcar jam-packed with native passengers who invariably sit crosslegged, so that one has the painful illusion of watching electric coaches pass by filled with wretched amputees; an evil orchid branch jutting through a garden railing; two Hindu children fighting over an empty sardine can; a holy man meditating on the steps of the Victoria Memorial; tiny Bengal thrushes resting on the hilt of King Edward's sword.

My Bombay friends busy themselves so that I will see the things in India one reads about in books and sees in pictures. They do exist. As a result I shall perhaps take part in a tiger hunt courtesy of Monsieur Lebaut, the renowned agent of the famous Hagenbeck Zoo; through the good offices of Doctor Faraglia, a physician well known here in Bombay, I will attend the dance of a *bayadère* from one of the Brahmin families virtually inaccessible to Europeans. For three days they have been wanting to take me to visit the Tower of Silence. But nobody has died.

Today, Lady Harvet, a striking elderly woman whose

blue eyes provide the only color contrast with the white of her dress, face, and hair, walks into the reading room of the Majestic Hotel. She is ecstatic. "He's died!" She is followed by her son and Doctor Faraglia, both of whom also exclaim, "He's died!"

"He died last night, the architect Donald Antesca-Cabisa, a Parsee of some importance. The funeral will be held today at six P.M. You're in luck. We have time to take a drive to the Esplanade and climb Malabar Hill to watch the ceremony. We'll have lunch at the Tower's gardens. We've brought along provisions."

Before you know it we are in the car driving at top speed (I, who would so much rather go on foot, savoring the joy of treading new ground the first days here) and the city whirls past like a motion picture run far too fast.

Now we are at the Esplanade, where the huffing and puffing of the automobiles and the pawing of the equipages blend with the shouting of a crowd composed of ten different races and the sound of twenty military bands. This is the promenade, the Bois de Boulogne of Bombay: interesting, varied, and as illogical as a futurist painting. All the vehicles—hackney cabs drawn by humped zebus with gilded horns; elephants caparisoned to the ground with sumptuous velvets, under which all that can be seen are four enormous feet, the mutilated tusks, the trunk, the ears constantly in motion like two gigantic fans; carriages drawn by horses of the purest white, preceded by panting, shouting heralds: inside recline the wife and daughter of a high English official, and the lady's fairness (she is clothed in the latest European fashion) creates a strange contrast to the exotic and archaic magnificence of the retinue, the turbans and velvets of the coachmen and the bronzed nudity of the heralds.

The car of a rich Parsee, the car of the bishop of Bombay, with a prelate on either side, smiling and unabatedly blessing with his raised hand those worshipfully kneeling or bowing in the crowd. At this hour of the day the city recalls fabled Babylon, Alexandria, Rome, or Byzantium, despite the wheel tracks, automobiles, and Paris fashions. It exudes a feeling of wealth and abundance. It includes a sense of inevitable, childish envy, of unjust ill-feeling against rich, powerful England, which rules half the earth.

After the English, the masters of Bombay are the Parsees. The Parsees, not to be confused with the Hindus (I even mistook them for the pariahs—one's ignorance is abysmal when one suddenly travels twenty degrees of latitude without preparatory study), not to be mistaken for the Moslems or Afghans, who are as different from one another as a German is from an Arab. The Parsees are descendants of the ancient Persians who emigrated from Persia to India after the Moslem conquest. Truly biblical and grandiose is the destiny of these followers of Zoroaster, who, rather than have to renounce their god, the Sun, left their native land twelve centuries ago; they arrived in India as persecuted refugees, seeking refuge first in Diu, then Tabli, where they negotiated with the maharaja to be allowed to settle in peace. They were, however, sorely molested for almost a millennium, and their peace and prosperity began only with the English conquest. The English recognized their qualities, which they encouraged and protected. The largest capital investments in Bombay are in Parsee hands. The Parsees control a large part of political life; the Parsees produce the best businessmen and university graduates. Still, no one is more traditional than the Parsee, no one less affected by Anglomania than he. The Parsees dress as they did a thousand years ago when they fled Persepolis—the men, in broad white robes and high black tiaras similar to miters (which strike the newly arrived European most); the women draped in brightly colored silks—sulfur yellow, pale lavender, cherry red, violet, willow green—which throw into relief their jet-black hair and amber pallor. As their mode of attire is millennial, so, too, are their faith and its rites—the doctrine of Zoroaster, inspired by the religion of creating and conserving elements, most of all the sun and fire, the symbol of the sun on earth. England, which tolerates all creeds, also tolerates the Tower of Silence and Parsee funeral customs, which are surely those least reconcilable with our Western sensibilities.

We climb Malabar Hill. The city grows steadily smaller, only from above can it be seen in its entirety, and one enjoys the panorama the way one does Naples from the height of Posillipo—a Naples three times larger, stretched out between the mountains of Deccan, the Bor Ghat, and the Arabian Sea, and crowned by wild vegetation bathed in a light intolerable under our skies. The automobile climbs along the reddish road, drives in the shade of the coconut trees, the banyan trees with their multiple roots rising, descending, and multiplying their trunks into infinity. We reach the top of the hill, an immaculately kept garden bordered by great beds of Bengal roses. We take our place under a veranda crisscrossed by strange, huge bellflowers, and suddenly the portable

table is out, the provisions are taken from the automobile. Lady Harvet arranges the culinary wonders—twenty products from every clime—in which the enviable English appetite delights: milk, honey, tea, local and European jams, pickles, relishes, candied and tropical fruits. I scoop out a fruit, a mangosteen, which you eat in its peel like an ice, cutting its excessively aromatic sweetness with lemon juice. I look around me: the delightful garden that dominates Bombay has been spoiled by the gas company, which installed a gigantic storage tank among the palms.

"A gasometer? That is the Tower of Silence. The others are smaller *Dakmas,* used only in case of plague."

I am greatly disappointed.

Tower of Silence: the Shelleyan name promised not this whitewashed cylinder but the most imaginative object the poetry of death has ever sculpted from stone. The tower is surrounded by a waterless moat, over which two bridges are suspended; they lead to a small—indeed minuscule—door, the only opening in the white mass. Suddenly, a large shape, black and sinister, appears between the structure's gleaming white and the blue sky—the first vulture, then a second, a third, then six, seven alight on the Tower, adding a dark ornamental motif to its bleakness. The griffins of death truly exceed every expectation; one would say that nature has equipped them according to their dark destiny. They have immense wings, powerful for flight, made for the abysses of the sky; yet in repose they let them hang next to their bodies, trailing them obscenely in the dust; formidable talons, but without the noble profile of the eagle's, talons made for sinking into putrid flesh, not for struggling with live prey. At the base of their breasts, above a thickly plumed neck, another animal is grafted: the trunk of a naked serpent, yellowish, wrinkled, with a bald head, a dark beak, and eyes whose gaze, which alternates between insatiable ferocity and melancholy cowardice, is unbearable.

The *Dakma* is covered with vultures no longer meditative but excited, with their winding necks extended toward something new. Along the road, halfway up the hill, the funeral procession shines white between the tawny dust and the green foliage. Everything is immaculate, shining white; a strange custom the very opposite of ours, which shrouds the sorrow of final farewell in black.

"Are we going to enter the Tower?" I ask rather anxiously.

"No one, not even the Emperor, may enter there. Only a special sect of gravediggers and the accompanying Dastur are allowed to enter."

"The design is quite simple." With a pencil the doctor draws an amphitheater divided into three concentric circles, subdivided by radii that form a large number of small open cells. "Here, the inner circle, the small cells, are for babies and children; the middle one for women; the outer one for men. This is the central pit where they collect the cleaned bones, which an underground aqueduct carries to the sea. Barbaric logic? Why barbaric? For the Parsees, fire is the manifestation of God, indeed the godhead itself, as the consecrated host is for the Christian. They therefore shrink in horror from committing corpses to the funeral pyre as the Hindus do, so as not to offend the godhead with putrefying flesh. They shun burial because the *Avesda,* their sacred book, forbids them to leave the body, which is the agent of the soul, to decompose slowly in the earth. The vulture, the sacred bird of the thousand-year-old rite, is perhaps best suited to annihilate the wretched dead substance and return it to the life cycle."

The procession approaches. Perhaps twenty persons, dressed entirely in white, with their heads and faces hidden by snowy veils. Four bearers carry the supine corpse, covered by a light shroud under which can be seen the pointed shoulders, fine profile, and thin legs. The followers are bound in pairs by a twisted handkerchief: the funereal *crati,* emblem of kinship in misfortune. The scene is very simple and grandiose, almost devoid of sadness. At the first bridge the column comes to a halt, as if by common agreement, and only a few white figures follow the corpse: the closest blood relatives—mother, father, a brother. The litter is set down before the open door; the followers stop for a few seconds in front of the corpse, perhaps for a farewell prayer. Opposite them is the Dastur, the Parsee priest, with two assistants. No one else: no groans, no tears, no tragic gestures. Perhaps the Parsee religion, like that of the Brahmins and the Buddhists, expunges all sense of the Oriental self, and their millennium-old philosophy eases the agony of separation with no return. The litter has disappeared through the little door, which has silently closed. The white shades return two by two, still united by their funereal cloth. They leave it, as the rite prescribes, without looking back, and disappear among the palm trees.

Yet high above in the air there is a dense, fearsome swirling of black shapes. They approach from the azure heights, grow larger, dive with the speed of a falling stone, the funereal griffins. Against the blue of the sky, the gleaming white of the Tower, the dark wings seem attracted and repelled by the hostile whirlwind; they make me think of the large wings of fallen angels. But there is no cry, no struggle—only a plaintive and subdued shrieking, as if afraid of awakening someone.

I experience a slight shudder. I feel horror at the agony I cannot see.

"A splendid chap. He had the makings of a talented architect, he'd already won a competition for the Health Museum building. His uncle, the solicitor Makalla . . . "

An architect, a lawyer: men like us, who studied our books, assimilated our formulas and ideas, and were able to reconcile them with remote feelings repugnant to our sensibilities, like those of the bloodiest savage. The abyss between men seems to me every bit more terrible and unbridgeable, and the world seems more shrill and ridiculous and absurd. Ridiculous and absurd the Tower surrounded by tall palms, between telegraph and power poles, ridiculous and absurd this automobile; and we too are ridiculous, who stop on this slope as if it were an airfield, or an Occidental hippodrome.

"There is no suffering. The corpse is picked clean in twenty minutes," Doctor Faraglia explains to me, biting into his third sandwich, "and picked clean with truly religious delicacy. The skeleton remains intact in its cell, composed as if prepared for an anatomical laboratory. With a single peck of their beaks, they open the cranium where the frontal bone joins the nape of the neck."

"Your friend hasn't eaten or drunk anything," Lady Harvet remarks politely. "You won't be able to tolerate the Bombay climate unless you eat twice as much."

Elephanta Island

G ARAPURI, "City of Caves," or Deva Devi, "Island of the Gods," is perhaps the most beautiful excursion Bombay has to offer. Surely there is more exotic interest for foreign visitors in this small area than anywhere else in the Indian metropolis. Yet rarely does an Englishman, much less a native, suggest it to his guest. Instead it's off we go to the spectacular skating rink (yes, they have the courage to pursue this sport with the thermometer showing a minimum of thirty degrees Centigrade) or to Cléo De Merode's exclusive appearance at the immense Esplanade Cinema, where to the (alas, futile) whir of thirty fans I feel a jolt of homesickness when watching the sympathetic smile of Robinet against the backdrop of Valentino Park. No, this isn't really why I came to India. It is by no means easy to play the perfect tour guide to one's own country. Even the most beautiful sights close at hand are no longer perceived. It would never occur to the English to show you Elephanta Island, just as we Italians hesitate to suggest the Baedeker tour of Capri, Monreale, or Superga. The English go to Elephanta for two reasons only: to eat and to court. The launch that covers the six nautical miles from Bombay Island to Elephanta Island carries mostly picnicking families and lovers—a journey to the Land of Plenty, *embarquement pour Cythère.*

Today isn't Sunday; the steam launch is almost empty. It isn't Sunday, and the huge port of Bombay, not paralyzed by the inexorable holiday rest period, offers the whole joyous, multicolored panoply and varied beauty of its activities. We have to cross the harbor of the great Asian metropolis; the launch passes like a tiny buzzing gnat among the hulls of ships from all over the globe— English, French, Dutch, Japanese, Australian, American—ships of every period and size: some huge, new, untouched, impressive evidence of the state of the shipbuilder's art; others of archaic form, of indefinable age, immense rafts with a single large sail, which dare to cross the Indian Ocean to Africa and back, entrusting themselves to a special monsoon on a certain day; decrepit sailing ships that give the Isthmus of Suez a wide berth because the tolls at Port Said vary from thirty thousand to one hundred thousand lire and more, consequently repeating the centuries-old voyage around the southern tip of Africa; round-bottomed ships of a uniform hue of old rotten wood, with yellow, tattered, patched sails so dilapidated they recall the Portuguese galleons that first sought shelter in Bom-Bahia—Bombay—from the slave-traders and pirates who for centuries were the undisputed masters of these lands and seas.

It isn't a legend. The entire sailing and fishing population of Bombay, which lives on the nearby islands in tiny hovels beneath the shade of lofty palm trees, is descended from pirates. The island of Colaba, outlined in green beyond the forest of masts and sails, was still inhabited by shipwreck hunters at the beginning of the century. Their villages are said to have been built entirely from the salvage of wrecks. Picturesque uncouthness and victorious civilizations, all races and tongues, every line and color, mix and clash in this international rendezvous that offers so many rare sights to the connoisseur of anachronism and paradox.

We sail past a newly arrived English steamship. The curved black hull rises above us to dizzying heights like the side of a colossal cetacean. We hear voices from the innumerable portholes, impatient faces appear; down the all-too-precarious gangway travelers descend to a landing launch; four naked Hindus receive the baggage, help the children and the unsteady as they jump. A blond lady balks, the travelers urge her on from behind, encourage her, protest; a swarthy giant picks her up unceremoniously, hands her to another likewise naked giant, who puts her down delicately and unscathed in the boat between her neatly stacked luggage. The woman screams uncontrollably; the bystanders laugh. The blond woman's white arms clinging desperately to the barbarians' shoulders make me think of a Roman woman during the last years of the empire: a *flava coma* hotly contested by two slightly irreverent Nubian slaves.

The whole port exudes a bearable servitude: the masters are haughty but just in exploiting men to their last ounce of strength. Black shapes teem on the ships, from ship to ship, on taut ropes, on rope ladders, and on piles—low-caste Hindus come and go, filing past one another in opposite directions, like orderly lines of ants; or rows of them hand along, from one to the next, huge baskets of coal, bales of cotton, bunches of bananas, and crates of spices. Oddly enough, this wretched, lowly people has an innate gracefulness, a harmoniousness in gait, gesture, and carriage. As throughout the Orient, they all sing while they work, a slow, close-mouthed melody that grows more pronounced and rhythmic when they strain, producing the not unpleasant effect of a monotone, buzzing symphony. Some of these wretches are women; they wear nothing but a loin cloth, though it is hard to recognize them as women. Almost all of them appear old: time and toil have collapsed their breasts, made their shoulders angular, their arms rough, their whole person masculine. Are they unhappy? Perhaps not; certainly less unhappy since the Europeans delivered them from the oppression of caste. Almost all of them, you see, are pariahs, that is, "beyond salvation," inferior to crows and dogs, beings one could kill with impunity since they exist outside the cycle of evolution, excluded for all eternity from any hope, damned in life and death for the sole sin of having been born. Now the majority of them wear the scapular on their bronzed chests, rough and unsure but consoling; they have in their hearts the idea of possible salvation, the hope of being able to claim from death that which life has denied them.

The endless port gradually vanishes behind us. The forest of steamers, sailing ships, and junks thins out; several rafts still drift on the tinlike sea, often punctuated by the dorsal fins of sharks and schools of flying fish. Sea and sky blend into an even, limitless, colorless calm. One has the impression of sailing on the void, in prehistoric times, when the seas brought forth plesiosaurs and giant ferns.

Then, all of a sudden, as if drawn on a crystal panel suspended in space, the island of Elephanta appears, a patch of solid green. Farther off, the tawny-colored strip of terra firma crowned by the chain of the ghats: Bor

Ghat, a lofty wall of crimson basalt, a martial glacis carved by nature into towers.

It is ten A.M., and it is already so hot that the speeding launch provides no relief. Despite the double awning, the sun burns brow and cheeks like a brazier. A *boy* armed with a pump douses the deck and awnings with seawater, but the moisture's patterns disappear instantly in the tropical January heat. Never have I been so glad not to be overweight as in this climate: India is truly infernal for anyone with a few extra pounds.

The heat creates mirages, dissolves the air, makes it quiver and flutter on the horizon along with the shimmering of the tide alongside. Already near, the island of Elephanta doubles, is reflected fourfold, approaches, recedes, and disappears.

When it reappears, we have arrived.

We land on large granite cubes, slimy with red and blue algae abandoned by the high tide, hanging down like the hair of unknown sirens. The hill rises steeply out of the sea. There are two items of interest on the island, not the lunch and love of the Sunday English, but the vegetation and the famous temples. For the first time since being in Bombay I observe the license of the tropical flora. The magnificent backdrop of Victoria Gardens, the Esplanade villas, and Malabar Hill was designed by expert gardeners after English models, and each tree trunk bears an oval plate with the correct Latin name: *Cinnamonum camphora, Vanilla aromatica, Ficus elastica, Stychnos nux vomica, Tamarindus indica,* etc., etc., a dreadful practice that lends a pharmaceutical air and the banality of a druggist's to the poetry of an exotic garden.

Here there is nothing but nature, a flora gone wild—

nameless and unrestrained. The beach is lined with huge pandanus, which extend their multiple roots into the water, raise their leafy crowns to the sky, and make one think of inverted candelabra or vegetable wading birds. You ascend the hill by way of steep stairs carved into the basalt by a Brahmin monk in fulfillment of a vow, for the benefit of the visitors. From time to time the vegetation intertwines above our heads and forms a green corridor in which the sun's rays tremble as in an underwater landscape. Among the white, supple trunks of the coconut trees, and between the straight trunks of the Palmyra palm, is a tangle of vines that join the forest from tree to tree and make the islet a patch of greenery floating upon the sea.

I would like to leave the path and go into the trees, into the refuge of the green night, but the *boys* and my friends are firm: it is the hottest part of the day, time for the cobras; for the holy island abounds with cobras.

Halfway up the hill, the famous temple comes into view. It is a hypogeum that reminds one of Egyptian structures and consists of a number of grottoes dug into black stone similar to porphyry. The columns multiply into infinity, hang suspended from the gloomy vault or rise mutilated like stalagmites. The temple is wrought with an eye for wonderfully painstaking and patient detail, though oblivious to proportion and the harmony of the whole. Despite all the damages caused by the millennia, infiltrations, landslides, Moslem and Portuguese fanaticism, the temple still presents a complete and impressive synthesis of the Brahmin Olympus—a highly complicated Olympus, hard to get straight if one has no special aptitude for untangling the numerous kinships involved.

The main grotto is dominated by a relief perhaps four-teen meters high depicting a fearsome body with three heads, the famous *Trimurti:* Shiva, the creator, Vishnu, the preserver, and Rudra, the destroyer. A trinity made flesh, metamorphosed in the bas-reliefs of the shady por-ticos into a thousand other figures of a confused symbol-ism. Here we have Shiva riding a bull, making himself simultaneously male and female with the male symbol *linga* and the female *yoni,* surrounded by an infinity of figures: elephants, tigers, serpents, sages, *rhisis, apsare,* the aurochs of the Brahmin Olympus; here is Indra, Brahma reclining on a lotus blossom drawn by four swans, smil-ing Vishnu flying on the back of a vulture with a human head. In the divine sculpture there's also Shiva, from whose face spring the three great rivers—Ganges, Jumna, and Sarawati—Shiva who enters into lawful marriage with Parvati, the slim-waisted goddess with enormous breasts, who embraces her spouse with one hand while strangling a rival in the shape of a female monster with the other.

There is a multitude of gods and demigods, relations and guests, votaries and servants, who offer food and refreshment on all sides. Another bas-relief depicts a gar-den: the celestial mountain Kailasa, overflowing with *sagas* and blissful women since the union of Shiva and Parvati produced Ganesa, the God of Wisdom, a mon-ster with an elephant's head and a tiny, rotund, pot-bel-lied human body. Again there's Shiva in a bas-relief showing the most distressing, bourgeois revenge a god can inflict upon a family. Shiva has married a second wife, Durga, daughter of Daksha, son of Bhraham, and procreator of sixty daughters. Daksha holds a ritual ban-

quet, assembles all the gods, but has unfortunately forgotten his son-in-law Shiva and consort. She interposes
herself in the ceremony and, being unexpected, is
received rudely. She throws herself onto the flames of the
altar. Shiva appears, and in his rage, with his multiple
and fearful rotating arms, decapitates his father-in-law,
his fifty-nine surviving daughters, and his guests, strew-
ing severed heads on all sides.

One grotto is dedicated to a *lingam* wreathed by yellow flowers. On special days thousands of Indian women
come here on pilgrimage, to kneel or sit on the rough
obelisk of stone and turn a number of times; the ceremony insures fertility. The temple exercises supreme control
in all things through the Shiva Lingam. This symbol of
procreation is strange indeed in a religion in which the
ultimate good is not to have been born or, having been
born, to be annihilated as soon as possible. Yet it is surely
my profane Western mind that does not comprehend the
hidden meaning of the sculpted stone. For example, the
tragically pessimistic figures found on all the entrance
arches, depicting armed men holding a grinning skull in
place of their genitals, send a shiver down my spine. The
impression of this oversized damp, dark, lifeless hypogeum
with its shrieking bats and constantly dripping water is
not religious but gloomy. These figures wielding clubs,
lances, and provided with multiple arms the better to
wound, figures that seem to jump off the walls to fling
themselves violently at poor mortals, express frightful
idolatry. I would like to ask these gods the reason for all
this frenzy and for the woe, worse than life or death, they
have reserved for wretched mortals.

Certainly, more than a dilettante, the European schol-

ar who comes here after having leafed through the Indian
holy books and experienced a few hours of solace from
the sublime speculations of the Vedas and the Upanishads is disappointed and indignant when confronted
with this barbaric, savage theogony. The fatal destiny of
all religions that establish churches and translate themselves into stone, metal, color, and form is, however,
idolatry.

Visitors to the underground tomb of Elephanta certainly do not indulge in such melancholy reflections: the
thirty breasts of the goddess Cassavi, the tiara of the
Asparas, the broad elephantine brow of Ganesa are covered with names, dates, hearts with arrows through
them, garlands of roses inscribed in pencil or carved by
penknife to immortalize fleeting love. Exactly as in the
West.

I WALK into the open, into the green jubilation of the
celestial island. I walk from shade into light, from bar-
barism into civilization, from the decrepit past into the
victorious present. Bombay is outlined on the horizon,
with its anchorages, archipelagoes, and peninsulas. From
no other vantage point can one better grasp the wonderfully balanced topography of this Asian metropolis. I
reflect, not without pride, on the miracle Western activity has accomplished in these infested swamps in little
more than half a century.

"The life of a man lasts two monsoons," the natives
told the first Europeans who landed. Today Bombay is
one of the healthiest cities in India, surely more salubrious than Calcutta, Goa, or Madras. But what a price in
human labor was paid for this gigantic process of

destruction! Two centuries ago, at the mouth of the River Ulas, the parallel crests of two submerged hills, far from the coast, extended into the sea; the intervening space was filled with brackish lakes and jungles occupied by wild beasts. The Portuguese explorers considered this bog to be hopelessly uninhabitable. John IV of Portugal gave the archipelago of Bombay to his daughter Catherine, upon her marriage to Charles II of England, as an insignificant dowry; Charles leased it to the East India Company for the unbelievable sum of two hundred fifty lire per year. It became a place of refuge; they tried to populate the damp and infernally hot region. Yet it wasn't until the final annexation by England that the future city began to grow on the insalubrious archipelago. The swamps and jungles were drained and destroyed, and the two hills joined, forming today's island. A few of the large gardens maintain specimens of teak, of the centuries-old palms, survivors of that wild flora: civilization respected them as it respects the columns of the Indians' temples, created large gardens around the venerable trunks, and forced the wild beasts to live inside cages. Where fearsome antediluvian landscapes once stood, well-groomed flower beds now flourish, fair-haired babies play, followed by native nannies, by a mother, a sister who shows off the latest European fashions. An excellent orchestra answers the roars of the caged tigers with a melody by Verdi or Wagner.

From atop Elephanta Island—tomb of the past—one contemplates the island of Bombay, cradle of the future. No contrast is more significant or profound. Oriental philosophy and Occidental philosophy with their opposite conclusions: a dark, fearful temple of idolatry versus a flourishing metropolis overflowing with abundance. I think of the warning of the macabre phallic symbols: it is better not to have been born.

Better not to have been born. But having been born, to take things easy with all the goods that life can provide.

The Dance of a Devadasi

Thanks to the good offices of Doctor Faraglia, this evening, as the guests of a traditional Indian family, we will attend the dance of a Devadasi, a high-caste *bayadère*.

The word *bayadère* evokes utterly false images to my Western mind fed by adventure stories, oleographs, operas, and operettas. *Bayadère, odalisque, houri*—that is, an Oriental lady, preferably brunette (except when the soprano has a fine head of bleached-blond hair), dressed in an Oriental costume equally suited to Thaïs, Semiramis, Cleopatra, or Salome—two jeweled cups, fine for their absence or irritating presence, some sort of tulle sheath attached to the thighs and knees by a tinseled encumbrance, and two insolently European legs, clad in pink silk and two ankle boots à la Louis XIV. You must forget this fashion plate and, most of all, the notion that a *bayadère* is immoral.

A Devadasi (handmaiden of the goddess), that is, a *bayadère* of the Brahmin caste, boasts noble lineage going back thousands of years, because she can only be the daughter of a *bayadère*, just as her children must be *bayadères* if female, and musicians and poets if male. It is easy to understand how a Devadasi may come by her refined art of gesture, gait, carriage, the voice and the

mask, and the literary attitude that enables her to penetrate and uniquely comment upon the masterpieces of
Indian poetry.

Born and raised in the temple, reared in accordance
with the strictest regimen, she has no need to learn the
sacred languages of Sanskrit and Pali, familiar to her
from infancy; the strophes of the *Puranas,* the heroic and
sacred Indian poems, are her bedtime reading as a small
child; her first steps move instinctively to a dance
rhythm, her first words to a rhythm of song and poetry;
her lovely dark eyes are scarcely open before they reflect
the fabled architecture of the holy enclosure, the gods,
heroes, and monsters of stone and metal, her officiating
and dancing sisters in ceremonies and processions. A
prisoner in the temple up to her fourteenth year, her
horizon is circumscribed by the pond of sacred crocodiles
and the high walls guarded by stone elephants. She is
raised in religion body and soul. She is born into and
lives a mystical fairy tale. Her entire education aims at
fashioning her into a living temple sculpture.

As soon as she reaches puberty, the flower of her beauty may—indeed must—be plucked by a protector of
noble birth, a nabob who is linked to her officially by a
sacred and indissoluble bond. He must endow the
bayadère with a large patrimony, recognize her, include
her in his will immediately after his wife and before his
children, and pledge an annual offering to the temple.
This bond does not exclude, indeed inaugurates on the
part of the *bayadère,* a way of life that seems to us the
most shameless of infidelities; because from that day
onward she is assigned to the cult of Rama Devi, the

Venus of the Indian paradise. She participates in inde-scribable ceremonies and is offered by the priest to all the faithful—of high caste—who pay an adequate offering, an offering that goes to the temple treasury and not to the Devadasi.

Alas, at this point a Westerner is utterly perplexed, and thinks that in his own country a temple, a priest, a priestess of this sort would merit a less arcane and cer-tainly less respectable name.

It is all a question of latitude—latitude in space and time. Twenty centuries of Christianity make us blush in shame or smile a malicious smile at such customs. Brah-mins do not blush, nor do they smile, just as the pagan who arrived in Paphos and Amatunda to offer the obol to the famous temple did not smile or blush. It is a well-known fact that the Greeks and the Indians have the same origins, the kinship that united Brahmin to Hel-lenic theogony. Over the centuries, Rama Devi, dusky Eros, armed not with arrows but cobras, has become the Venus of the Indian paradise, the undisputed sister of the Greek Aphrodite who survives in the land of Brahma while the other has vanished forever with the advent of her nemesis—the Virgin Mary.

We, worshippers of the Mother of God—affirmation of the spirit and negation of the flesh—are unable to comprehend an erotic religion. Our entire inner being, clothed in a morality two thousand years old, is shocked and rebels when confronted with the sister of the ancient adversary from the mists of the ages.

For this reason we are unable to comprehend or define a Devadasi. In addition to being a consummate actress, a scholar, a devotee of poetry, she is also a possessed priestess, a crazed maenad.

But we blush from shame, or smile maliciously.

Do NOT laugh or smile, do not refuse the garland of jasmine around your neck and the essence of roses on your hands, do not offer your hand to the mistress of the house, do not praise the beauty of his daughter or of his consort to the master of the house, etc. Doctor Faraglia expounded a set of injunctions to us against every possible breach of good manners as we traveled in the moonless night in a small native carriage drawn by zebus—the thin, highly agile Indian oxen with tattooed hides and long, backswept horns painted gold. There are fourteen Europeans in my group. We are going toward Calam, on the Travancore outside Madras, under a vault of lofty coconut trees that show a profile even blacker than the black of their fronds. Above and below there is a dust cloud, a flickering of stars and fireflies, an intense perfume of unknown flowers nourished by a recent monsoon. A winter night every bit as sultry as our hottest August nights.

A palisade—we enter a garden preceded by two servants who light the driveway with a large acetylene lamp. Strange, vivid, heart-shaped, lancet-shaped leaves appear; zinc vegetation, painted tin, velvet, and baleful flesh, the intertwining roots and winding branches. An Indian garden is identical to the jungle except for trimmed plants and the paths spread with multicolored gravel, arranged in geometric patterns, which the patient gardeners renew every day. The house at the end of it doesn't look like the abode of a Hindu multimillionaire—a low whitewashed building with sloping verandas and wooden colonnades, which would remind me of our rural train stations if they weren't framed by the green flabellum of Palmyra palms and the vegetal jet of coconut palms. We are received in the entrance hall, served (to our great surprise) champagne and whiskey and soda, which, with delicate irony, the master of the house has had brought from the distant city to slake the thirst of the impure with their impure drinks—the same master of the house who would not accept a glass of water from us and will certainly put aside, for other Europeans, the glasses we have drunk from.

In all honesty, I did not expect to find India so untouched. Everywhere outside the large cities Brahma rules, Brahma who has ruled for the past two to four thousand years. The master of the house, a Hindu in his fifties, comes toward us followed by his son. We both bow with our hands pressed against our foreheads. They are dressed in nothing more than a strip of cloth around their hips, yet their entire naked persons exude a nobility far more impressive than the impeccable fancy dress of European high officials. They ask us questions about our business, exchange a few polite words in English, smile, showing their brilliant white teeth between their red lips and their beards divided in the center and brushed back. But their magnificent eyes are absent, cold, and impenetrable. The son offers us a few sheets printed in Hindi characters, with, on the back, a typewritten (!) translation of the sacred program.

From tall engraved silver cruets a servant pours essence of roses on our hands; other servants, in the way we deck Christmas trees at home, place woven garlands and gold tinsel around our necks. This looks like a fairy-tale custom, though it is the tribute most frequently met with all over India, in the big cities as well as at receptions attended only by Europeans—a delicate, poetic custom. To be sure, these long boas of large, fragrant magnolias that look so stunning around the neck of a young English girl are laughable on a gentleman's evening jacket. For example, they make the ruddy, pot-bellied Dutch consul look like the caricature of a mother-in-law.

We walk across the garden to the theater. We are late. The masters of the house do not come with us. Why is that? Faraglia explains to me that this is the third evening the *bayadère* is performing, and all castes are welcome to attend, including those with which a Brahmin is not permitted to come into contact. So this is why we have been admitted. Very flattering indeed!

The real Hindus, those who honor the past and are immune to Anglomania, possess the art of opposing European arrogance with a pride far more implacable and haughty, concealed beneath the most cordially urbane etiquette. The theater at the end of the large garden is a simple, large shed supported by the living trunks of symmetrical palms, as if by slim vegetal columns. Many benches crowded with bronzed torsos surmounted by raven-black hair, many mats on the ground and on all sides. A large shed, more a storage place for lumber or grain than the venue for a *bayadère* who earns a thousand rupees (sixteen hundred lire) a night.

The dance had already begun when we took our seats on the front-row benches set aside for us. It is my fortune to have the famous dancer directly in front of me, but a few steps away. I had expected to see her completely naked, or almost; instead she is wearing more than most of the audience, and she is certainly wearing more than one of our respectable European ladies at a soirée. She is slim like Ida Rubinstein, though one is hard put to say whether her figure is embellished or encumbered by an unusual costume of silk, velvets, and superimposed tulle that leaves her shoulders and arms bare. Yet from her shoulders to her throat, from her shoulders to her hands, gold and gems gleam, real gold, real gems, as prescribed by the monastic rule, an entire treasure that sparkles and glitters on her fine brown skin—yellow gold from the Coromandel; Mannar pearls, rubies, emeralds, and sapphires from Ceylon; and from the fabrics, the gold, the gems, all that emerges naked is the composed mask of her face, her hands, and her perfect feet. And her face! I couldn't take my eyes off it. In a race in which everyone—men, women, old people, children—seems to have been chosen by a jury of artists, approved and improved by a beauty parlor, one can understand the miracle of flawless harmony a *bayadère* can attain: a specimen produced by thousands of years of selection. Her face would truly be too beautiful, the eyes too large, the mouth too small, the profile too regular, too similar to a kind of Indian miniature I consider mannered, if the perfect mask were not animated and agitated by the emotions of a soul in torment. The mimic play is so expressive that for a few seconds I fear the woman is furious with us. Yet it isn't rage, but pain, deathly dread that expands and contracts the fair mouth, flares the trembling nostrils, and knits the great eyebrows. It is the face of one on the point of death, contracted by a fearful vision. Perhaps—I read the action of the various passages sung and mimed in the program—the Devadasi has shown us the atrocious pain of the dying Maharani who is being carried to the holy Ganges on a golden litter, sees death approaching, and fears that she will not arrive at the purifying waters in time.

The Devadasi does not dance, she moves forward and backward to a static rhythm, following the music and the strophes. There are, in fact, some musicians—I hadn't seen or heard them, so taken was I by her acting—seated on mats playing enormous mandolins with long, curved necks, tapered flutes, and strange oblong drums, which they shake feverishly. Still, the overall effect of this formidable ensemble is a humming as light as the fluttering of dragonflies and moths. No one sings, but all, musicians and audience, chant sotto voce the verses of the sacred poem the *bayadère* is repeating to herself, as if to remember them or by common agreement. One hears and sees nothing except the oval mask, the triangular smile, the overlarge eyes extended by eye makeup all the way to the veils of her compact, gleaming hair, which seems sculpted of rare ebony—a mask that seems to detach itself from the person, to become a separate appendage, like a spiritualistic evocation. Her hands are truly wraithlike, like those that wrote the condemnation of tyrants on the seas in biblical legends. The hands of this Devadasi, at the ends of her immobile arms, toss with a dizzying rotating and twisting motion that seems to defy every law of anatomy. They have, I was told, the important function of signifying scenery and stage directions. Instead of the scornful paucity of scenery in Shakespeare, cards saying "The Forest" or "The King's Palace," objects are drawn with the art of two lovely hands, are drawn in the air but remain imprinted on the eyes of these excited spectators, who create the invisible background for the artist. On the wretched reed-matting curtain appears the fabled royal palace, the banks of the Ganges, the Indran heaven. Unacquainted with this art, my profane gaze cannot, of course, enjoy the spell, just as I cannot understand a single syllable of the famous text—the woman's mime alone suffices to reveal to me the instant in which the dying queen reaches the river shore and descends into the holy waters. The pain and anguish are transformed into a joy that turns the contracted face into a mystery of ineffable delight. The dying woman revives and invokes the Brahmin Olympus in a strophe so erotic it could surely not find seemly translation into a European language. Her mimicry is so intensely expressive that I feel a thrill of love and death run down my spine. The woman lets her head fall back, raises it again; her face is calm, she has left the wheel of existence and has arrived in the realm of the impossible, the no-longer-being—grace has been granted to her in the arms of God. Once again I remark the predilection of Indian art, literature, and sculpture for uniting love and death, fusing the two into a single symbol: the happiness of not being born or, having been born, of returning to nonbeing.

The audience of perhaps a thousand persons has followed every syllable and gesture of the Devadasi with a concentration unknown in our European theaters. Not only attention but passion and religion transport these souls toward the wealth of their poetry. Poetry! Imagine an actress of ours inflicting a book of Homer or Virgil upon an audience, a public audience—let us say it once and for all—bored to death when it hears Dante, a poet not that far removed from us in time, declaimed by even the very best of reciters. It is marvelous to see how a poem three or four thousand years old can stir the fervor of everyone in a large audience: the spice dealer and the maharaja, the urchin and the simple woman. All are brought into the same magic circle, assisted by an illusion which is not literature, but an artistic, hereditary feeling that borders on and fuses with the most intense belief. Art and faith expressed by the same harmony, a felicity we Occidentals may never know.

After the last syllable the Devadasi lands on the carpet with a leap. She sits down with the sigh of relief of a youngster at the arrival of recess. We are seated around her respectfully, but her face reveals a complete spiritual emptiness; the music has ceased, as has the flame within, and one really has the impression of approaching a spent lamp, an instrument that has ceased to resonate. Doctor Faraglia—the only one among us who knows Hindi—compliments her on her art. The woman is slow to understand, then smiles, covering her face with her raised forearm as if she were a convent schoolgirl to whom a brazen lad had whispered something forbidden. I, who do not speak Hindi, point to her swollen left cheek. She brings her index finger and thumb to her lips and pulls out a lump of vermilion matter, which she offers me.

"Betel!"

When I decline the awful drug, she pops the plug back into her mouth, shifting it from one cheek to the other, clapping her hands in jest like a mischievous child.

"Tell her that I deeply regret I did not understand a single word of her poems. Ask her how many years it would take me to learn Sanskrit, Pali, and Jain."

The woman listens to the doctor, then looks at me intensely, and with a laugh raises all ten fingers. Ten years! Alas, no! It isn't worth the toil. Then I think that even after having mastered these difficult languages I would remain forever alien to the sacred texts. There is a barrier between us more insurmountable than that of language: the different spirit and opposite faith. The Westerner who returns to India no longer recognizes his cradle. I am well aware that these Hindus are Aryans of our stock, our brothers; but we are brothers who refuse to reach out in one another's direction. We are too different. Too many millennia divide us. We said farewell to one another too long ago.

Goa A Dourada

No one wished to accompany me on my excursion to Goa. My friends stayed in Bombay, fascinated by the many pleasures of the hospitable metropolis.

Go to Goa? Why? There are many reasons, all indefinable, indeed almost impossible to admit; they simply speak to my deepest longings as a wandering dreamer. Because Goa is not mentioned by Cook or Loti; because it is the port of call for no shipping company; because an unforgettable sonnet by Heredia urges me thither; because few names captured my adolescent imagination as powerfully as Goa: *Goa A Dourada*.

I visited it with my pencil a hundred times during never-ending math lessons, with my atlas open between desk and knees. Here I am sailing between the Isthmus of Suez and the Red Sea, entering the Indian Ocean; now I am circumnavigating Africa on a sailing vessel that touches the Cape Verde Islands, rounds the Cape of Good Hope, stops at Madagascar. In my peregrinations a companion (whom I haven't seen since) followed me; he had every right to be aboard the ship of my imagination. He had a brother who was a missionary in Goa, a brother he had not seen in years, whom he almost did not remember, but to whom he owed an enviable album of colonial postage stamps and several letters that spoke of Malabar and the Ghats, of tigers and Saint Francis

Xavier, and some photographs of the cathedral and of the mission set between swaying coconut palms. Postage stamps, letters, photographs, and a name—Vico Verani— all these are etched in my memory as if I had beheld them an hour ago. To me the voyage over the pages of the atlas seems to be living reality, and this sea and sky, pale imaginings—sea and sky of molten tin, bordered by the Malabar coast, a strip of green.

Once again I muse that our feelings toward things are nothing more than the poor offshoots of a few seeds planted by chance in our pitiful brains during early childhood. Today my voyage traced on an atlas twenty years ago is coming to an end, coming to an end upon this heaving teapot, a caravel with a rounded hull, thirty meters in length, in which has been installed what is doubtless the first steam engine ever invented. Yet this is all unutterably poetic, and more than compensates for the specious elegance of the great modern steamships with their cabins and presumptuous staterooms filled with mirrors and stucco à la Louis XIV and à la Bona- parte, which smell like ordinary hotels, without the slightest trace of seafaring poetry, a sense of adventure, and the unheard-of.

Here everything is poetic. I can imagine myself living during the age of Vasco da Gama, sailing to *terrae ignotae* and *insulae non repertae*. I sleep in a small bunk near a porthole that looks like an eighteenth-century window. Scorpions, cockroaches, and termites are everywhere, but this fact is redeemed by the pictures and statuettes of the saints that surround me, from Our Lady of Assistance to Saint Francis Xavier, with strange Portuguese prayers against shipwreck; the wood in the cabin smells of salt water and decay, and creaks at night to the rhythmic gnawing of the termites.

There are only a few passengers: a handful of Goan merchants and five monks returning to Goa from the Northern Missions. I had hoped to hear some news about the unknown missionary:

"I am going to Goa to visit the brother of a friend of mine: Vico Verani, Velha Cidade."

None of the five monks has heard of him.

"We are from the convent in Panjim; Panjim is Nova Goa. But I know all the monks at the Cidade. I will give you a letter of introduction for Father Jacques of the Basilica of Bom Jesus, another for the cathedral."

These Goan monks look strange, with their angular, earth-colored faces, their broad smiles and small eyes, black as onyx chips inlaid beneath their great bushy eyebrows: Zuloaga figures exaggerated by the climate and crossbreeding. Their laughter, looks, and gestures are all very lively, the very opposite of the stiff bearing and light complexion of the neighboring English.

TODAY I went into the hold. What a collection of ill-assorted cargo it contains! Pianos, typewriters, bicycles, bales of cotton cloth with vivid floral patterns for colonial belles, three enormous crates containing a huge statue of Saint Francis Xavier disassembled into three parts, a gift to some Portuguese convent from the bishop of Bombay, and an endless number of sacks filled with bits of broken pottery. Broken crockery is collected by street sweepers all over the West, vividly colored fragments eagerly sought by the Goan mosaicists, who use them to compose beautiful pavements with complex designs.

I am pleasantly surprised. In the galley, between a bunch of bananas and a tin of canned goods, I have found a book: *Os Lusíadas,* The Lusiads, the immortal epic poem by Camões, an incredibly soiled old edition with the *alvará régio,* the permission of the licensers, at the bottom of the title page. I do not know Portuguese and find the little Spanish I have of scant help, yet the verses are so harmonious and the rhymes so perfect that at the end of each strophe I feel I understand exactly what the poet has meant. I am also aided by the cook, the scullery boy, any sailor I can find: the epic is as popular among the illiterate as *Bertoldo* and the *Reali di Francia* are in Italy, except that *Os Lusíadas* is one of the most perfect masterpieces of the European Renaissance. It is the Portuguese national literary work—alas, all that survives of the colonial greatness of those splendid days. With good reason, and not undeservedly, Camões was called the Portuguese Tasso. All the elements of the great epic are brought in to serve the figure of the hero, Vasco da Gama, and his discovery of the East Indies. Still, I am unable to read it without an irreverent smile. The figure of the Portuguese Ulysses is so grotesque, filled in according to the classicizing mania of the times: one can almost see the boots, the patched outfit of a medieval pirate showing underneath his cuirass and the helmet that echoes of Homer and Virgil. The entire pagan and Christian Olympus presides over the feast. The Virgin Mary on one side—an excessively paganized Virgin—and Venus on the other—a Venus who smacks of the sacristy and the Holy Inquisition—contend from time to time for the navigator-hero.

The poem opens with a storm at sea in the ancient

style when Vasco da Gama rounds the Cape of Storms. Bacchus harasses him, Venus protects him. A landing at Malindi, reception by the king and his daughters, and a generous hospitality, which Vasco repays in three long cantos by retelling the annals of the Portuguese, their past and future glories, with an endless, rhetorical list of the names of all the ancient heroes when they arrive at the royal palace. Now we have Dido disguised as Inês da Castro, and the moving account of the departure of Vasco and his fleet, and the Cyclops, parodied by the giant Adamastorre. And, after all these Homeric and Virgilian echoes, Vasco arrives and conquers Goa, takes possession of the rest of India, not forgetting to draw up a formal treaty with the various rajas in harmonious octaves. The navigators return home in triumph and are received on an enchanted island, an allegorical paradise where the nymphs of Thetis, wounded by Venus, repay them for their hard labors. The saints of the Christian paradise join in with applause—what a peculiar book—for the goings-on upon the academic lawns of this Garden of Armida.

A peculiar book indeed. Yet full of beauty; and it is certainly the most poetic viaticum for the dreamer sailing toward legendary Goa, the one best suited to whiling away the hours of tropical torpor, lying on one's back on deck under the double awning in the monotony of a seemingly unending voyage.

Vasco da Gama is one of the most mythical names I know, so much so that I am unable to see the man without the legend, am incapable of picturing him as a living mortal on this sea under this sky which was his. Yet his fleet may have navigated these very waters when with great pomp he welcomed aboard his accomplice and ally the negus. And the emperor of Ethiopia and the Portuguese captain bent over the charts to contemplate an enterprise worthy of the Cyclops, a revenge fit for a demigod: to divert the course of the Nile so as to force it to issue into the Red Sea, destroying rival Egypt for all time by drying up the valley and its delta. Perhaps Vasco had this scheme ever in mind when the explorer arrived for the last time in this land of his glory and torment, a prematurely old man, misunderstood, at death's door; and, when the calm of the Indian Ocean was convulsed by a sudden earthquake, the dying captain gave courage to his petrified crew, crying out in a firm voice: "Fear not! It is the sea that trembles before us!"

ALAS, the sea is not trembling before us. Three days of an unvarying scene. Sea and sky the color of molten tin, with here and there a streak of black: as always, the fins of sharks upon the horizon, silhouetted against the only trace of anything tangible, the thin, wavering strip of light-green land—the Malabar coast.

I WENT up on deck at dawn. We are working along the coast. The green has risen like a curtain extending into infinity. These are the coconut trees, the trees that rule the entire coast of Malabar, Ceylon, and Papua. Monotonous and dense, they take root all the way to the beach, where high tide encircles their trunks with seaweed and anemones. These are the coconut palms, the dominant visual feature of these regions, the wild palms that lend the tropics their nostalgic note. I can't understand how my traveling companion can call them dates, confusing them with the columnlike trunk of the African date palm—all scales, fibers, and metallic fronds, arid companion of pyramids and deserts. The coconut is the friend of the pagoda, the son of dampness and hot shade. The trunks stand out white against the greenery, oblique, thin as the stems of fantastic weeds, shooting the green rocket of their foliage twenty, thirty meters into the air, gigantic, undulating with an infinite grace on their too delicate boles. Leaning against the rail with my chin cupped between my hands, I gaze for hours at the enchanting beauty of this unique scene. I did not expect to find a most Christian city hidden beneath the lush shade. The *Pedrillo* has sailed up the estuary of the Mandovi River, set us ashore at the shaky *imbarcadero* of the Velha Cidade, and hurriedly left for the Nova Cidade lest low tide strand it on these shores.

For two hours I have been walking around the strangest and saddest of ghost towns. The Orient is full of once existent cities that go back thousands of years to the dawn of Buddhism and Brahmanism, lost in the abyss of time, race, and religion. Still we find in Goa the specter of our own civilization: sixteenth- and seventeenth-century convents, palaces, and churches, a vast city that at times reminds one of a street in baroque Rome or a square in Umbria, a city once sumptuous and wealthy, which rose by command of the cross and the sword, a city that once contained three hundred thousand inhabitants and now numbers three hundred. They are now all monks or caretakers of the crumbling palaces and churches, apathetic witnesses who do not restore a single stone, resigned to the implacable attrition of the climate and the forest. As to men, the tropics are deleterious to things, and beneath this burning hurricane sky the centuries count as millennia. The city is endless, but few of the buildings are still whole.

I walk haphazardly, without a destination, without a letter of recommendation, escorted by a lively urchin who questions me about my choices: "Palace of the Inquisition, Chapel of Saint Francis Xavier, Cathedral of Our Lady of the Elephants?" and he begins to consider my absentminded wanderings with some misgiving. One building attracts me, an imposing seventeenth-century palace with curved window gratings, pretty balconies, and volutes bearing in the center, in italics, a monogram or proprietor's coat of arms; the coat of arms is also reproduced in stone in the vast entrance hall. The inner court is surrounded by a baroque open double gallery with spiral columns. At least half of the open gallery has collapsed and one sees the wild countryside above it. I wander along the arcade, enter the vast dwelling. Alas, I gaze up at the ceiling, and through the ceiling at broad patches of blue: the tropical sky. There is no trace of the three landings, of the interminable suites of rooms and corridors. Everything has tumbled down, and the palace is nothing more than a box, a deserted rats' nest used as a storehouse for coconuts. On the ground, up to the height of several meters, are piled the large, hairy fruits, which make me think of pyramids of severed heads. I walk outside, sit down under the portico on the base of a broken column, and quench my thirst from a coconut the caretaker has cracked open and handed to me.

"Whose palace is this?"

"The abbot's."

"No, I mean who lived here, who had it built?"

The caretaker does not understand me, gives me a perplexed look. I point to the coat of arms, which can also be seen showing here in the worn pavement.

The man doesn't know, shrugs his shoulders indifferently.

"Who can say? A conquistador—long, long ago."

Which conquistador? Is it possible for three centuries to wipe away to this extent all recollection of our earthly passage? The recollection of powerful men, of feared and envied conquerors who filled the world with their names and deeds, who imposed their names with the cross and the sword, engraved in marble and iron on their magnificent palaces?

Was it Diego Lejnez? Alfonso Dequero? Manrico Tizzona? Perhaps I have already met these scowling eyes in some European gallery, in a portrait by Velázquez or Van Dyck, one of the conquistadors, half-trader, half-pirate, warrior and explorer, who advances in all the pomp of silks, plumes, and velvets, holding his consort by the hand, a plump lady with symmetrical curls, smiling in spite of her iron corset and cruel gorget; and the offspring, all proper, all corseted and armored like their parents; and a Negro slave carrying a monkey on his shoulder and a parrot in one hand, with the other holding up a velvet curtain; and between the two columns the mighty fleet lies at anchor before the fabled city: Goa, *A Dourada,* Queen of the Orient, pride of the sons of Lusus, where the sun never set on the Portuguese dominions. "Whosoever has seen Goa need not see Lisbon."

Once again I am disappointed and pay the price of wanting to see the reality of the dead stones too close up, wanting to verify, to ascertain that the things glorified by art and history, sung by the poets, no longer exist, will never again exist, are as if they had never existed. Endless streets, in which rundown palaces hollow as skulls alternate with wild greenery that has overgrown massive old walls, towers cloaked in hanging tendrils, swollen lianas spotted like pythons; and churches, religious ruins sadder than the profane ones. I take a rest in the cool shade of a fragment of a vault with an ogee arch left miraculously intact, supported as it is by a lone surviving wall. For one homesick instant I cherish the fond illusion of standing in a dilapidated church in Romagna or Abruzzi. Then three obscene monkeys—truly apocalyptic symbols of Satan—occupy the hollow of the apse, a flock of tiny parrots runs across the four arches. Animating the dead stone there is no ivy, no familiar insects, but a strange creeper with yawning flowers and diabolical, cross-eyed chameleons. From above, a coconut palm has extended an immense frond into the church, where it slowly waves, projecting a shadow on the ground like a hand imparting a blessing.

The melancholy of the dead *cidade* is utterly unlike that of a medieval European city, this part of our past being buried in a savage land underneath a sky of exile. I have no goal, I have nothing to guide me in this solitude of plants and ruins other than the name of an Italian I never knew. I repeat it to every one of the few passersby I meet, but no one is able to tell me which convent is his. There are many convents, and I walk from one to the next in vain: nobody knows Vico Verani; without his religious name it will be difficult to find him, and I do not know that name. Several people suggest I talk to someone in the cathedral, where the registers of the ecclesiastical office are kept.

I quicken my pace, followed by a Goan urchin interested in my search. He brings out loud exclamations accompanied by grotesque gestures, rolling his eyes and waving his arms excitedly, excessive mimicry revealing that he is the offspring of a bastard race. We arrive at the center of Goa: more solitude, silence, and death; formidable as a fortress, the palace of the Most Holy Inquisition, an institution more frightening than its European parent, and one primarily responsible for the decay of a colonial rule of unequaled greatness.

This is the cathedral, abbey church of the Indies, a mosque converted into a Christian house of worship by Saint Francis Xavier. And this, on a deserted square shaded by palm trees, is the Basilica of Bom Jesus. I visit the tomb of the saint, a sumptuous baroque mausoleum of jade, marble, and silver. The body of the saint was officially declared Viceroy of the Indies and Lieutenant General; the actual governor, who arrived from Portugal, had to solicit the idolized body's approval. Until the beginning of the nineteenth century, he still came to this church in great pomp to assume his post, for the rites required that he return for a conversation with the holy reliquiae prior to making any important decision.

The monk has me proceed to the sacristy: we cross a vast, walled inner courtyard in which the squat style of ages gone by, the centuries-old melancholy, creates a strange contrast to the greenery and the blinding sky. We mount to the second floor. In the library I am introduced to the Father Superior. The monk receives me kindly, has three or four registers from different periods taken down from the shelves, leafs through them quickly and carefully, points at the yellowed paper with an index finger bearing a large violet-colored stone. In the silence I consider his bespectacled face beneath a gray tonsure, the heavy person in the black-and-white tunic, and the other companion, silent, lean, stiff, posted beside an ancient planisphere with figures of beasts and savages inscribed on its borders. At the padre's back, behind the high-backed armchair, the large window opens onto a tree-lined courtyard in which a group of native urchins, whose faces seem even darker in contrast with their white shirts, are performing gymnastic exercises to the accompaniment of a kind of liturgical chant. The smell of rancid incense, aromatic tobacco, time and sanctity; the smell of unfamiliar flowers and foul tropical odors. I am having a nightmare. I look with anxious impatience at the index finger that descends the page of the huge register. The silence seems to last forever. I would never have thought I would be so anxious to meet an Italian, especially the unknown brother of a forgotten friend.

The Father Superior stops. Finally, he reads: "Father Miguel, in the world Vico Verani, Convent of Santa Trinidade, instructor of theology beginning September 20, 1884, ordained in 1891, and . . . "

The father lifts his face, and his serene eyes look straight at me.

"He died on October 22, 1896."

Silence.

"No one lasts very long in this climate, dear sir."

The solitude seems more complete, the desire to leave more insistent, now that I know that I have been following the trail of a dead man in a dead city. The monks propose their hospitality. They insist. It is ten kilometers to Panjim, the Nova Cidade, where I can find a hotel. Night will fall when I am halfway along the road. No matter. I say farewell. I board a zebu-drawn trestle, a vehicle resembling a bier or a tub, in which the traveler lies down almost on his back, raising or lowering a sort of cradle hood over his face.

In a whirl we're off to modern Goa.

MODERN Goa looks like a provincial town from past times, a capital of a banana republic at the end of the eighteenth century. I spend the evening in the most banal way possible in order simply to convince myself that I am still alive and in the present—I go to a motion-picture theater. Then I walk to a café surrounded by a large throng, so different from the correct elegance of the English and the dignified grace of the Hindus, a crowd of Portuguese *mestizos* who in this climate reproduce like weeds, who have outlasted the ruins, more stubborn than the stones, and who pompously call themselves *Toupas*—that is, Europeans "who wear hats." Yet there is nothing European about them, with their delicate bones, their slight legs, their angular, olive-hued faces with vivid simian eyes under their prominent brows. They have a grotesque chivalric bearing, are well-groomed and pomaded, smoke huge cigars, and have languid female companions who display the fashions of a decade ago, remainders shipped to them by a European department store.

I sip a small glass of arrack, the national liqueur and

the colony's principal export item. Amidst the deafening, rough, incomprehensible shouting and the smoke that blinds and suffocates me, I write picture postcards to some European friends. I notice that the stamps still bear the likeness of Don Carlos; the florid mien of the slain monarch smiles at me from behind the crude surcharged correction in big black letters: *República*. . . . I don't know why, but this detail closes this Portuguese episode, a melancholy day among the most melancholy of my pilgrimage, with a final sadness.

I leave the café, take a stroll in the gardens. I continue on along the seacoast, where the gas lanterns stop and all the stars of the tropical sky appear, dominated by the Southern Cross. In the darkness you hear the characteristic rustling of the palms in the breeze from the sea. I try to remember and repeat, like a prayer over the tomb of the dead city, a sonnet by Heredia for his native land far away.

Morne Ville, jadis reine des Océans!
Aujourd'hui le requin poursuit en paix les scombres
Et le nuage errant allonge seul des ombres
Sur la rade où roulaient les galions géants.
Depuis Drake et l'assaut des Anglais mécréants,
Tes murs désamparés croulent en noirs décombres
Et, comme un glorieux collier de perles sombres,
Des boulets de Pointis montrent les trous béants.
Entre le ciel qui brûle et la mer qui moutonne,
Au somnolent soleil d'un midi monotone,
Tu songes, ô Guerrière, aux vieux Conquistadors;
Et dans l'énervement des nuits chaudes et calmes,
Berçant le gloire éteinte, ô Cité, tu t'endors
Sous les palmiers, au long frémissement des palmes.

More than in Camões' rumbling academic epic, Goa A Dourada is contained in this miracle of fourteen verses.

The Garden of the Lord

THE Indians aren't the masters of India. Nor are the English. The rulers of India are the animals, especially the crows. One has this visual and auditory impression the moment one sets foot in one of the great capitals: Bombay or Calcuttta, Madras or Rangoon. Incredibly prolific, more prolific than the pigeons in Venice, the crows teem and blacken everything—in the port between bales of cotton and spices, in the beautiful palm-lined streets, in the great modern squares. They drink and bathe, flapping their wings in the vast basins; they form blue-black borders on the capitals of columns, on the cornices and spires of serrated Gothic-Indian buildings. If the vultures are the gravediggers, then the crows are the street sweepers of the immense empire. They are also its thieves, thieves made bold by millennia of tolerance that even the most zealous policeman cannot counteract.

The traveler who takes an elevator to one of the clean, tidy little rooms in the huge tropical hotels is astonished by the signs posted on its walls: Beware of Crows, Lower Blinds Before Leaving, Do Not Leave Jewelry Lying About, The Management Declines All Responsibility For, etc. This might seem unbelievable, but I changed my mind the same day. Here it is 10:00 A.M., the lazy siesta hour. The immense city is asleep: no one, not even a native, crosses the great square where the sun is blazing, blinding, tremulous, making the trunks of the palms, the Victoria and Albert monument, and the spires of St. Thomas Cathedral shimmer in a strange underwater landscape. In every room of the hotel a European dreams of his faraway country, lying on his back, underneath the coolness of a huge fan. Silence. The only sounds to be heard are the buzzing of the mechanism and the other noise that is the acoustic note of India, a sound one has to accustom oneself to as in countries where the omnipresent crash of the sea predominates: the steady, monotonous, unbroken chattering of crows. It is a hymn to decay in which the entire gamut of *r* sounds erupts, in which the ear seems to distinguish the unpleasant words: Remember! Wrack and ruin!

"Yes, I am only too well aware of all that, you damned birds! But in the meantime we'd like to sleep."

Sleep comes almost immediately, yet almost as quickly I am awakened by a strange sound. Then, through my narrowed eyelids, I witness this curious scene: a crow, hitherto perched on the matted blind hanging at the large window, alights on the windowsill, explores the quiet room, and hops gently onto the floor. Another repeats these proceedings, and yet another. Four, five gentlemen jump cautiously down onto the floor. These crows (*corvus splendens*) are smaller than ours, svelte, jet-black, with a white feather on their wing tips, and make such droll movements with their funny shapes. They advance one after another, hopping cautiously, the one in front with neck outstretched, another ramrod stiff, on the alert, the next limping and misshapen—all like caricatures in a fable, personages worthy of Aesop or La Fontaine.

The crows enter kitchens and storerooms out of greed. It is the demon of curiosity, risk, and theft that have brought them into this neat, tidy room smelling of resin and fresh sheets. The five petty thieves halt in admiration, form a circle around the suspenders hanging from a chair, peck at the shining buckles with their beaks, tug at them until the suspenders and trousers fall off the chair and begin to wander around the floor pulled by five robust beaks. Then you throw something at them, a nearby slipper, the book you had fallen asleep with, hoping for a flutter of wings and precipitous flight. Before the missile reaches them, however, the crows avoid it with a hop, silently ascending, setting down in perfect order on the uppermost rod of the mosquito bar. You open all the glass windows, invite them to leave, threaten them with your—all-too-short—umbrella, but they cannot make up their minds. They know very well that you are not a Brahmin or a Buddhist and that you would mercilessly break their wings or skulls. Then you call the *boy* in desperation. The *boy* smiles indulgently; he asks you to put down your umbrella, claps his extended hands, and the five perchers, having identified the man as one who does not kill, cross the room one by one and silently exit.

In India all animals display an astonishing familiarity with man. The sparrows, the turtledoves, the striped squirrels invade courtyards and gardens, almost come to take the crumbs from your hand, filled with a Franciscan trust; yet in the crows and monkeys this familiarity becomes the insolence of greedy calculation. No doubt they believe Bombay and Calcutta were built for them and that man is an intruding biped to be endured with ill-concealed rancor. Man in his turn tolerates the crows in the great cities; they clean the streets of all filth before it decomposes under the blazing sun, tearing up, swallowing everything, even rotten paper, bits of rags, bits of glass. After a few days I find them pleasant; watching them, one is treated to priceless scenes and strange demonstrations of animal psychology. Surely no bird is more cunning; one merely has to observe their behavior toward different people. Toward evening, at five-o'clock tea, when every public and private garden, every hotel and bungalow veranda comes alive with silk veils and other garments, blue eyes and fair hair, the black phalanxes descend from all sides, clucking, garrulous, and muted, like beggars. They surround the tables, swirling, hopping, each with extended beak, far enough away to elude your grasp, close enough to quickly snatch a biscuit or a banana peel. They sense whether or not they will be well received; they do not approach men, avoid walking sticks and umbrellas, preferring the tables of women and children.

With the natives they are not beggars but despots. In the native towns beyond the European cities they live almost cheek to jowl with man, enter his houses heedless of uneasy threats, secure in a millennial pact that rules they are not to be killed. What priceless vignettes they provide in the native suburbs! A toddler—a tiny bronzed idol not quite three years old—comes out of a shop holding a cup of boiled rice and runs toward her mother, who is waiting at the door of the house across the way. Halfway across the street twenty crows are suddenly upon her; not in the least frightened by the circle of flapping wings, the little girl hugs the cup to her body, bending forward, raising a part of her that is not exactly her face toward the sun, against the greed of her enemies. Her mother arrives, liberates her child, disperses the attackers, though not without first having dispensed a handful of rice as a bribe. Both return to the house, smiling calmly, as if it were a well-known joke between old friends. Other times the victim is an ape rather than a tot. The crows swarm on high, spying a group of monkeys that have stolen a coconut from a nearby market, follow their leader, who has taken it from the others, and the instant the thief brings the white pulp to his mouth, the crows dive on him, wrest away the treasure, and leave him snarling at his squawking companions, empty-handed.

The monkeys contend with the crows for control of the Indian cities, but do not infest them as they do the European quarters. They live in the suburbs, in the black towns and temple ruins, where the tenant farmers hate them more than they do the crows. A herd of these quadrumanes can take the top off a house at night, removing all the roof tiles for fun, passing them from hand to hand, piling them in some cellar or on top of a hill a few kilometers away. Sometimes they sack a garden, stripping it of everything—unripened fruit, flowers, and leaves—simply out of a nasty destructive instinct. They are also the tyrants of the markets, where fruit vendors resign themselves to losing an exorbitant tithe of their wares. Dusty monkeys loiter on all sides of the pyramids of bananas, mangoes, mangosteens, and *cati,* swirling, ready to reach out a paw heedless of the little boy on guard. During the evening, the gutters of all the long suburban streets are decorated with hanging tails. But if a European walks by or an automobile drives past, anything out of the ordinary, the tails disappear, giving way to an equal number of snouts outstretched toward the road, teeth gnashing in a frenzy of curiosity. An infinite variety of creatures is tolerated, protected, or venerated in this great garden of the Lord. On the windows of the hotels, even the most elegant hotels, great hump-backed insects with suckers on their legs run upon the glass, and the hotel manager tells you not to disturb them. The Bengal thrushes, red speckled with silvery white, teem by the hundreds on the verandas and in hallways and come to peck at the crumbs under the tea table; the mongooses, looking like tawny weasels, walk warily along the corridors, guarding, by virtue of a strange gift of immunity, human lives against the most terrible of guests: the *naia tripudians,* the black cobra.

What about the most pleasant creatures of all, the elephants? They complete the Indian landscape, are hard workers, possess a touching kindliness and a bewildering intelligence. Deluxe elephants destined for nuptial or religious processions are tattooed every color of the rainbow, like cordovan leather, caparisoned in velvets and heavy silks, with nothing of them showing except their tusks, trunks, and striped ears. The work elephants are yet more intelligent; some of them are ancient, with wrinkled, worn hides too lose for their frames emaciated from a century or more of toil, elephants who have beheld three or more generations of men and who today work for the houses of the fair-haired usurpers. They meet along the country roads, in pairs, unaccompanied by a *cornac,* travel ten or fourteen familiar kilometers at a slow trot, transporting unaccompanied huge tree trunks, columns, and blocks of granite upon their backs or between their tusks. They deposit these at their destination and retrace their long path at a brisk pace or pick up another load. You can hear their steps from far away, a dull rumble. If they come across a European, they retreat, step off the road, leave the way free, and, if it is already free, they extend their trunks expectantly. If they are given a small coin, an *anna* or half an *anna,* they stop at the first country shop, where they put the coin down in exchange for a heap of moldy rice or rotten bananas. They possess a disconcerting intelligence: in the tiny eyes virtually lost in their huge heads one sees, by turns, an indefinable glimmer of scornful cunning and indulgent good nature. I am certain they understand what I say, sense what I think, and I do not know how to show them my fraternal sympathy: my hands barely reach high enough to caress their trunks, rough as trees, the lower tips of their ears, worn and torn like old leather caparisons.

There are other creatures, too, repugnant and noxious ones; the most dangerous are also the most venerated. The cobra, which Brahmin theogony has transformed into a marble and metallic symbol in every temple, is greeted with a special ritual of reverence and exorcism by the Indian peasant who encounters it along a country path.

Every temple has legions of turtles and ancient, venerable crocodiles in its ponds. The feeding of the sacred crocodiles is one of the great curiosities shown to foreigners, one repeated with the identical ritual in the temples of Jaissur, Ambex, and Tuadura. Followed by a servant carrying a basket of rancid meat, the keeper descends the stairs to the lowermost step and begins striking a copper disc, producing a deafening crescendo. Suddenly, the great leaves of the water lilies and nelumbus begin to stir and slowly rise; the frightening monsters appear between the red chalices of nenuphars, resembling the carcasses of ancient studded armor, with sparse, sharp, yellow teeth that sometimes poke beyond their awesome jaws. They swim lazily and form a circle in the water around the keeper, who throws them pieces of meat to which a cord is tied to prevent their being seized in midair by the kites attracted by the sickening smell.

The English, who have a boundless tolerance, tolerate this as well. They also tolerate the Animal Hospital in Bombay, the ne plus ultra of its kind, the greatest propounder of this Brahmin philosophy, so utterly different from ours molded by Christianity, which restricts all divinity to man alone and considers everything else on earth unfeeling matter, condemned and without hope. The animal hospital, a compound-park that cost hundreds of thousands of rupees, welcomes all sick animals so they can get well again or die in peace. No European can stand the sight and stench for very long: phalanxes of broken-down horses and buffalo; emaciated, lame, crippled zebus afflicted with dropsy, covered with sores and wounds; monkeys, dogs, cats, all blind, hairless, maimed—a pathetic parody of the Ark. Our Western piety rebels, asks contemptuously why these poor beasts aren't given the coup de grâce, put to sleep with a double dose of chloroform.

"Because one does not have the right to destroy life, no matter whose it is."

"But to live for what?"

"To suffer."

"To suffer for what?"

"To become, to grow, progressively to remove oneself forever from matter through the weight of matter, to extinguish the cycle of endless incarnations, the desire to return to life."

What if this were true? If we were truly not the masters of creation, as our religion promises? If indeed the worm, the dog, and man are nothing but different gradations of the spirit, of the same immanent force that pulsates everywhere, hesitantly moving toward an unpredictable goal of which we are ignorant and that is perhaps nothing more than the peace of the Uncreated?

And our response to this elementary rhetoric, rendered odious by a plethora of theosophical pamphlets but expounded in a very few words by this zookeeper with the ascetic face of a bronzed Saint Francis? We are unable to smile the way our Occidental pride would have us smile.

Golconda: The Dead City

IN two days the Indian Central Railways have whisked me from the verdant coast to parched earth, from Hindu India to Moslem India. Everything has changed. No longer the freshness of tree ferns and palms, but ghostly cactuses, agave with huge, century-old flowers, candelabra-shaped euphorbias that seem to support the blood-red vault of the sky on their immensely high, thin trunks. One no longer sees the bronzed beauties with uncovered breasts and faces, but severely veiled Moslem women; no longer the manes of Buddhist and Brahmin prophets and ascetics, but yellow, mauve, sky-blue turbans, henna-tinted beards, baggy trousers, and great gem-encrusted scimitars; no longer the light architecture of Anglo-Indian bungalows or the sharp line of the pagodas, but mosques and minarets, the white cubes of Moslem houses, the small multiple ogee windows protected by wonderful gratings made of a single thin slab of open-worked marble depicting a tree with flowers and fruits, a female dancer, or two peacocks refreshing themselves at a basin.

Hyderabad, gleaming white under a blazing sky. I really hadn't expected a capital so large and beautiful and gay in the midst of endless, barren Hindustan. Hyderabad is very much Moslem yet immune to the filthy decay that characterizes the other great cities of Islam; it has remained unchanged since the time of *A Thousand and One Nights,* without a trace of decadence or European invasion. Were I a king passing through, I would honestly believe that this multitude had put on the costumes of ages past and was play-acting to do me honor, not that this was their everyday appearance. Everyday life consists of needs. These people, however, do nothing out of necessity. All the shops beneath the arcades display the most delightfully superfluous objects: jewelry, silks, velvets, bronze and silver pots, curved slippers, engraved, gem-studded scimitars, newly dyed veils hung up to dry in the breeze, light as a melting cloud, aglow with all the most delicate hues; perfumes, essences contained in tall sealed pots or in odd-shaped jars labeled with arcane letters. And flowers, flowers in abundance—pyramids of magnolias, hibiscus, of decapitated roses which the merchants sell by weight, like fruit; the crowd strings them together on the streets, improvising their daily garlands, which are more important to them than bread: a strange multitude that thrives on colors, scents, dreams, and appearances. We are quite far from Bombay and Calcutta, from the big coastal cities, where our practical Western "busyness" has already been superimposed and reigns supreme.

England ensures an illusory independence to the Kingdom of Hyderabad—a kingdom three times the size of Italy. For what kind of independence can a continental state enjoy when it is encircled by Anglicized states ready to send in a huge army at a moment's notice? The nizam, ruler of Hyderabad, knows that instead of armies England sends sacks of grain, and that famine—by now endemic to this increasingly parched region—would return every year but for the boundless generosity of his surrounding keepers. Hyderabad continues to live its millennial fable, untouched after ten centuries, proud within all the elegance and refinement inherited from Baghdad, Persepolis, and Byzantium.

I return to my hotel stunned by the blinding light and overabundance of colors, humbled by this elegant throng in whose midst my Western figure in helmet and leggings must pass for the ghost of a beggar. I search among my letters of recommendation for the most important one: a letter of introduction to Xatar Nilgami, the son of the nizam's prime minister. I have not come here to visit Hyderabad, the living city, but the defunct city of Golconda, which slumbers a few kilometers away and whose walls one cannot enter without special permission.

"The prime minister," I am informed by the manager, "is away with his entire family. He has followed the nizam to London."

"To . . . ?"

"To London for the season," he confirms, nonplussed at my ignorance. "You can present your letter to other members of the court."

As we are speaking a servant presents me with the calling card of a fellow guest, a professor from Munich, who is sitting at the other end of the dark hall.

He introduces me to his wife and immediately begins to talk enthusiastically about our king. I had hoped this was dictated by the beauty of my country, if only by way of Goethe's divine poems, but the professor has never visited Italy, nor does he know the *Roman Elegies*. For him, His Majesty Victor Emmanuel II is not King of Greater

Italy, but Lord of Savoy, a leading international numismatist and his highly envied colleague in the field.

I am shocked. However, the professor is even more shocked at me when he learns that I know nothing of my sovereign's numismatic fame and am unable to tell him which volume has just been published of the *Corpus Numorum Italicorum,* the colossal work he is compiling.

"I have been here five months with my wife on research that would interest you Italians: I have found two sequins and a half-sequin with the face of the Doge Ludovico Manin. The Republic of Venice traded with the center of southern India at a time when this region was unknown to the rest of Europe."

I entrust my letter of recommendation to the professor. That very afternoon a strange court vehicle arrives in front of the hotel, an antique victoria with great oval springs, two coachmen on the coachmen's seat wearing yellow turbans, and two grooms on the sides wielding a long gilt flyswatter—strange equipage made up of a combination of old Western kitsch and Oriental opulence. There is an unbelievable display of servants in Indian cities. No respectable person can leave his house even for a short stroll without a retinue of servants, devotees, and clients; a gentleman's first duty to an honored guest is to place two followers at his side to make way for him in the throng by loudly crying out his name.

We take our places in the coach and drive through Hyderabad past white houses. The sky is furrowed by swarms of black crows, green parrots, and doves dyed bright colors. At the outskirts of the inhabited city a sign announces Golconda Road in five or six languages. Golconda. For centuries the wonder of Asia, the city of fabled diamonds and bloodthirsty queens, the renowned setting for novels of love and adventure. Golconda the great warrior and voluptuary, whose fame was spread in vague terms by explorers, by Flemish and Venetian merchants. As with Thebes, with Mycenae, and with all other deceased cities overpraised in the telling, I expect to be disappointed: I know I am approaching a ghost. But I am not disappointed. Even the road leading to it is worthy of a great past. Beneath the blue sky supported by the straight trunks of the euphorbias a landscape extends as far as the eye can see, a landscape showing all the suffering and voluptuousness or a nightmare, an unearthly landscape composed of partly worn, livid stone, dominated here and there by heaps of enormous smooth, curved boulders resembling giant wineskins or the backs of pachyderms. It is like walking on a lunar plain, and, indeed, here nature has created out of lifeless stone a scene more fantastic than the living forests of Malabar. Gradually, as one draws nearer, the boulders become larger and closer together; they form piles of hundred-meter-high pyramids, imitate the silhouette of unreal hills, broken here and there by brightly lit patches. The hypothesis of wandering masses has been discounted on geological grounds, so I really have no idea how these boulders came together in this immense plain. Hindu legend relates that they fell from Heaven, that they are what was left of the raw material in the hands of the Creator, who, for fun, rolled it up and threw it to Earth. To be sure, this gigantic piece of nature is the model of the taste for the improbable, fantastic, and colossal that marks Indian architecture.

Golconda. On the other side of a great dry riverbed rises the ghost of the dead city with its huge, pale walls, crenelated and open-worked with a unique art. We cross the riverbed. In the center, in stagnant ponds, a herd of work elephants vainly attempts to take its daily bath, sucking in water with their trunks and spraying it upon their flanks. We reach the opposite bank at the foot of the gigantic walls. Military genius has been aided by nature in such a way that it is impossible to distinguish where the work of the latter ends and the efforts of man begin. Man has covered fifty-meter-long boulders with a brick pavement, connecting them with vaults and ramparts, which are in turn united by huge gratings joined by hooks as thick as a man's arm. Truly fabulous treasures must have lain within Golconda for the sultans to have girt them round with such formidable defenses. We climb up the principal fort, a multiple boulder that towers over the defunct city, constructed in levels that descend from a summit crowned by a tuft of green trees, which astonish amidst so much desolation. The whole looks much like the plan of *The Divine Comedy,* with machines of war on all sides—archaic cannon which attest that the death of the city did not occur so very long ago. Golconda was still flourishing during the mid-eighteenth century when tales of adventure, *romans merveilleux,* were fashionable in Europe, when the fugitive Madame Angot arrived here to tempt the spent desires of decrepit sultans with her Western beauty.

What a profanation of memories! The overweening grace of the Parisian fishmonger pursues me while the German professor comments on the epic events and the famous monuments.

"This immense mosque is the Mecca Mosque, so called because it is an exact replica of the Arab sanctuary that Sultan Car Alpur wished to reproduce in this city. The one on the highest buttress with the soaring minarets is the Mosque of the Last Cry, which was meant for the offering of desperate prayers once an enemy had breached the walls."

"I don't see how a city like this could ever have been taken by storm."

"It *was* taken by storm. Too much had been said about Golconda's wealth. Aurangzeb, Emperor of Delhi, declared war on the city in 1684 and conquered it in 1687. The city was sacked and the inhabitants put to the sword, although the life of the sultan was spared by order of Aurangzeb. From him they had to pry the secret known only to him—where the fabled gems and the state treasury were that had vanished during the siege. Rubies from Oxiana, Tibetan sapphires, pearls from Ceylon, diamonds from Sambalpur and Carmur, lapis lazuli from Bavacan: there was talk of jewels, piled to the height of a man, walled up in an unknown cave along with the skeletons of the last guards, killed in order that the secret be safeguarded. Only the sultan knew its whereabouts. The poor wretch was dragged off to where the conqueror resided in Allahabad and subjected to the most subtle tortures: a group of executioners tormented him; a group of physicians had to bring him back to life when he was close to expiring. All to no avail. He suddenly gave up the ghost, taking with him into eternity the secret of the treasures he had amassed."

We walk along the fortified walls between crumbling

mosques and cannon half-buried by dust. These ancient palatial ruins are of a place conquered little over a century ago, yet they look as though their destruction belongs to a previous millennium. From atop the fort there is a panoramic view of Golconda: the gigantic winding walls still look whole and formidable yet superfluous, as they no longer have anything to protect. Within the vast perimeter everything is rubbish, stones, dust, and death. The tiny paradise at the top of the fort is reserved for death. The Indians' reverence for everything having to do with death has miraculously maintained this cemetery containing the tombs of the entire dynasty of Golconda, from Sultan Ibrahim to Sultan Abdul Hassan, from the fair Indian Bhima Mati to the fair Moslem Shanah Shah; odd Cufic-inscribed tombs painted blue with the lettering in white, each adorned with an ogee arcade and four tiny minarets with gold domes; vegetation of death in all directions: myrtles, cypresses, dwarf palms with flower beds of sickly blooms kept alive by water the faithful carry from a distant well, bucket by bucket, as if they were fighting a blaze. It is impossible to describe the sadness of this exotic cemetery, this field of death in the city of the dead.

Yet here too my spirits are lifted by the thought of the adventuress-fishmonger. Did she really exist, the one the legend calls Madame Angot? Did she really wander from Algiers to Constantinople to Golconda?

> A famous fishwife named Madame Angot
> To royal Golconda did one day go;
> For her the Sultan's love was so rare,
> To his five hundred wives she was beyond compare.

Alas, her tomb is not here among those of the sultans. She returned to Paris loaded down with money and jewels, to enjoy them in hard-earned retirement. What fabulous stories of her adventures she must have told her illustrious Parisian colleagues at the soirées of her venerable old age.

Madame Angot. Did she really exist? At this hour, within these walls, her gay figure is more alive than ever; it helps to lift any excessively Romantic sadness. Irreverence is advisable before revered ruins. It is better to mock the fatality that weighs down upon men and the world by humming tunes from a comic opera.

The River of Pyres

BENARES . . . the Ganges . . . ”

I have to repeat these two fabled names to convince myself that I am really moving upstream in a boat on the holy river with the spectacle of the venerated city before me.

"The Ganges . . . Benares . . . ”

I have to free myself of the memories of too many descriptions—from the delightfully archaic ones left by Marco Polo to the modern, sentimental ones we owe to Pierre Loti—in order to return to reality, to see the long-awaited thing with my own eyes. Reading and writing are to no purpose; beauty we do not see with our own eyes does not exist. Oscar Wilde is right. Yet before I knew how to read I had already dreamt about Benares. If I return to the very source of my memory I see the holy city in a Napoleonic woodcut in my playroom. The memory is so clear that the dream from back then seems a reality to me and the reality of today a dream.

"SLOWLY! Closer!" I keep repeating to the hurried boat-man.

You have to see Benares from the Ganges just as you must see a stage from the front orchestra seats. The interior of the city is an endless labyrinth of filthy alleys, a worthy breeding ground for all the world's epidemics.

The city was built on the river, extending all its beauty toward the deified waters.

My boat hugs the ghats, that is, the lowest steps of the huge stairway. The dry season exposes the city almost down to its foundations, and the immense blocks of granite, the squat temples, the elephant heads of the Ganesas, the multiple arms of the Shivas, the massive statues destined to immersion for many months of each year, are coated now and again by a reddish mud that has created a breathtaking glaze. The red patina colors the river city—up to a height of sixty feet and more it marks the waters' realm. After that, the inhabited city, with its fantastic architecture, begins. There are two thousand temples in Benares, built like a forest along the five-mile stretch the city occupies on the left bank of the Ganges: temples in the shape of Buddhist pagodas, with Brahmin spires and pyramids, rounded cupolas, Moslem minarets, temples shaped after Eurasian churches, synagogues— everything is tolerated in this "Land of Forbearance," so long as you believe. You shall not say that your religion is better than the others. Whoever claims to possess the truth does not possess the truth.

Before us is the familiar silhouette of the temples and palaces with their staircases, verandas, observatories, their infinity of windows turned toward the river; here are the strange pinecone domes so characteristic of Indian architecture. Most of these proud buildings belong to maharajas from faraway lands, residences for atonement. Just as during the Middle Ages princes went to the Holy Land to atone for their transgressions, so Indian lords now visit Benares once a year, or they retire there in old age to exalt their souls in sight of the River God, who absolves everything. Everyone knows of the belief according to which whoever dies in Benares and has his ashes strewn upon the Ganges is exempt (exempt even if he is an non-believer) from the torture of reincarnation and attains the felicity of the Uncreated. The sick, the disinherited, and the aged from every walk of life arrive from the most distant regions of the earth—from the equatorial forests of Ceylon, from the snow-covered peaks of Kashmir—to find peace in the arms of Brahma.

It is seven o'clock, the hour of morning prayer. The sun lights the uppermost parts of the buildings, obliquely, igniting what gold is left on cupolas and spires, where black, green, red swarms of crows, turtledoves, and parrots whirl to greet the light with a deafening hymn. All living creatures go down toward the river upon the spiral stairways between one palace and the next, descend the great staircases that lend the river an indescribably Assyrian or Babylonian quality: a varied, dense, incessant thronging of men, women, children, old and young, fakirs, pilgrims. All of them carry garlands of flowers: huge magnolias, gardenias, unknown blooms with a penetrating scent, all these strung like rosaries, and before entering into the water they throw them into the river for the daily ritual. Turbans, silks, and velvets are hung on bushes or under huge ribless umbrellas that look like odd mushrooms; the men enter the water almost naked, the women retain a long tunic that adheres to their skin after the first ablution and intensifies the amber of their flesh and the harmony of their wonderful shapes. All pray and meditate. Meditate upon what? My boat passes before them; we have to veer so as not to run into them.

But they stare at me without seeing. Their gaze is into the beyond, their souls lost in the abyss of the ineffable. This is a strange city, in which everyone believes.

Many here are not fakirs, not saints, not pilgrims, but men twenty or thirty years of age: vigorous and healthy artisans, merchants, soldiers, workers who climb back up the stairs to resume their lives, but who—twice a day, every day—descend into death, lap themselves daily in inevitable death. Compared with them we are an odious lot, we Westerners, we bourgeois who ignore everything having to do with the soul, deride every science of the spirit, curse God, and flaunt an atheism rendered more hateful by our cowardly repentance in our final hours.

An infinite multitude that constantly renews itself, the magnificence of dark and light bronze, of marvelous forms. But not everything here is youth and energy. The features of old age, of illness, and of death so necessary to perfect Buddhist meditation, offer a contrast beneath this magical sky—an indescribable contrast. For it is well to remember that the greater part of this throng has come here to die, "to die in the best of health," as the good oarsman explains to me with a dreadful oxymoron. All the cruelest sufferings with which the destroyer Shiva returns poor human flesh to nothingness are gathered on the banks of the luminous river, offering the visitor a strange collection of samples as interesting as the new flora and fauna: scabies, leprosy, tropical eczemas (*framboesia, albinite,* etc.) that cover the bronzed skin with regular white patches, with others that are vermilion, or with undulating black-and-white stripes; horrible wounds, tumors that have eaten away a thorax, baring the livid heartstrings, or eaten away the cheeks, revealing the white dentition in a sneer one will never be able to forget; elephantiasis that bloats the legs, chest, the pudenda to an incredible degree, so much so that the victim seems to disappear behind huge leather bags of himself and is unable to move without the aid of some other worshiper. A group of these wretches is assembled around a still-young fiery-eyed holy man with a brown beard divided in the center: what can that seer preach to console such misery, to still the moans of that nameless heap of corpses? Perhaps he is repeating to the dying the words of the Enlightened One: "The wise man rejoices that his flesh disintegrates just as the impatient prisoner rejoices at the prison that opens its gates. Blessed be the music that leaves its instrument forever, blessed the flame that leaves its torch, blessed the soul that quits the flesh."

WE continue onward. The sermon is not for us. Today more than ever before I feel a slave to appearances, passionately enamored of everything that is form, shape, color, shade, and light: living beauty, the prey of death.

The city is endless: more temples; more towers, terraces, staircases. An infinity of votive garlands and vivid blooms float on the river, on all sides; jewels, teeth, dazzling eyes, the gleaming black locks form a mosaic of living specks between the reflection of the water and the splendor of the sun, as in certain Impressionist paintings. The eye grows weary. We move into a restful shaded area along the interminable *ghati*. Upon the granite blocks the slow waters have left a border of scum. A sinister stench of rotting flowers, putrefying flesh, fever-ridden dampness and pestilence reminds one with a shudder that this single hotbed has from time to time over the centuries been the source of cholera and the plague, the worst scourges on the planet. It is not surprising. Here a dead palm trunk has formed a dike against which a pile of decaying rubbish is accumulating: garlands of over-grown blooms, which the water converts into a stinking, slimy mass—peels, papers, rags, smoldering coals, branches, a white bone, a human tibia that the oar brings slowly to the surface, a pitiful leftover that has escaped a too poorly fueled funeral pyre. A little farther on, the Maharani of Kandaba is making her ablutions under a baldachin held by four turbaned servants. Around her women are holding her clothes, her necklaces, the immense breast strap of gems, while the august sovereign—a plump, elderly woman—immerses her sagging flesh in the river, makes a cup of her hands, drinks the foul water, alternating each sip with a brief gesture of offering to Heaven. Still farther on, a few small children are running and laughing, looking for bits of wood and charcoal in the refuse; several women, with one hand steadying shining copper amphorae and with the other hand on their waists, move toward the shore, swaying hips emphasizing their provocatively elegant gait.

Farther on, we pass before another platform of funeral pyres—there are many of them, but almost all are deserted at this hour. More temples and palaces tower above them like feudal castles. A strange city unchanged over the millennia, unchanged in its stone and in its faith. There are other fabled cities in the world to thrill the imagination, but they are specters of their former selves. Today Benares is exactly as it was during the night of the Aryan era, when they were celebrating Dionysian rites in

Greece, when the Arval Festivals were held in Rome, when Thebes offered sacrifices to Ita. At that time Benares already shone on the banks of the River God as it does today; then as now, her throng went down into the holy waters to meditate the mystery of becoming.

Another platform extends over the river, another series of pyres; but they are almost deserted in this salubrious season. What a heap of flaming corpses the plague must supply to these banks when it rages!

We approach the berth. Two corpses are floating in the river, tied to a rope, billowing in the white shroud for the last rite of ablutions. Another has burned so far as to be by now beyond recognition; only its two feet protrude from the flames; contracting, the toes spread open as if in a final spasm. They will be the last to be consigned to the fire, as it is the custom to leave the feet outside the pyre, symbolizing the final farewell. These funeral pyres are not lavish.

Our imagination conjures up lofty heaps of faggots, billows of smoke enveloping everything in fragrant eddies, solemn prayers: the pyres of martyrs and poets. There is nothing of the sort here, where simplicity borders on squalor. The pyres are diminutive, similar to small cots or to masonry stoves barely large enough for a human body, and you would think the fuel parsimoniously expended in this country of huge forests. And in these attendants, what perfunctory indifference! Over there a body is being removed from the river in a sort of grated stretcher, is laid out upon the cement cot between two layers of meager sticks. A Hindu pours on a small can of resinous oil; another lights it. The pyre flares up, and on the four sides undertakers clad in white jackets and turbans, armed with long rounded spatulas to push back the crackling brands, oversee the cremation. The four gentlemen in white bending over the modest brazier with these strange spoons make me think of four busy cooks, and there is nothing tragic about them. But, here as elsewhere, is the utter indifference of the Indians vis-à-vis a corpse, the absolute lack of veneration for the body once the soul has left it forever. They have a single hurried concern: to give it over to the flames, to return it to nothingness as quickly as possible. Not far away, around each funeral pyre, is a curved granite seat where the deceased's family sits. But there are no tears, no heart-rending farewell; the kinsmen attend the cremation to make sure the rite is carried out to the letter, that there is sufficient wood, and that all of the ashes are committed to the river.

A third corpse has arrived: a handsome boy, perhaps twelve years old, smitten by a sudden death, to judge by the calm look of placid sleep upon his features; his arms, yet unstiffened by rigor mortis, hang loosely, and his head with its blue-black hair lolls back on the shoulders of his bearers. A man, perhaps his brother, and a woman still young, perhaps his mother, take part in the ceremony, exchange a few words with the assistants, discussing, surely, the resin that the woman is sniffing: it is not good enough for them. The young boy waits stomach-up on the pile, his perfect profile, the dark edges of his lids undercut by the white enamel of his half-closed eyes, rendered more delicate by the sleep from which there is no awakening. An undefinable sorrow grips my heart as I stare at this adolescent face, stare at the other face of the venerable old man already dissolving in the flames. Perhaps I recognize in the one and the other—through the remote analogies of a single race—the faces of boys and old men who have been dear to me. We love the face, this mirror of the self; we love the wrinkles, the white hair of the aged, the blond hair, the serene eyes of small children. We are unable to conceive of the return of the dear departed without their faces, their smiles, their voices. Our religion (with one of the most medieval and infantile of dogmas, it is true, but I would rather not discuss it) satisfies this illusion of ours by promising the *resurrection of the flesh*.

How far they are from us! Before they are born, before they die, they have already said farewell to one another. Since the age of their Aryan origins they are serenely resigned to this despairing certainty. "Nothing is, everything is becoming." Because if things were not that way, the calm of this young mother who arranges a little ebony elephant, a tiny mill, and a scroll of paper (prayers, or perhaps pages from the notebooks of an eager schoolboy) would be monstrous and revolting. She does all this without a tear or a twitch in her face. Surely she is a perfect Brahmin, much better than the maharani spoken of in the holy texts who rent her hair, screaming over her son's corpse. The Yogis, it is told, sought in vain to bring her back to reality, to tear her away from illusion. So great was the woman's torment that the fakir succeeded in returning the soul to the body already laid out upon the funeral pyre. The mother threw herself on the revived boy, crazed with joy. But the little prince raised himself up on the pile, thrust the woman away with a groan, and said: "Who is calling to me? Who is tormenting me? Where am I? Who has broken within me the harmony of the Wheel? In which of my endless incarnations did I have this madwoman for a mother? Take her to the exorcist! Mara the temptress howls in her!" The lad then fell back and his soul departed for the ineffable. His mother, the Maharani Kritagma, went all the way to Anuradhapura, the Buddhist Rome in the center of Ceylon, to do penance, and enjoyed the supreme grace of being enlightened by Gautama himself, as the poet Kalidasa recounts.

The Empire of the Great Moghul

THE gulf between Brahmin and Islamic India steadily widens the farther north one travels. Islam has an undeniable predilection for desolate lands: deserts and steppes. In India as well, it occupies the vast central and northern regions which are delineated by the borders of the parched provinces. For the India of lush vegetation is a stereotype bred in adventure novels. The dense tropical forests, decorative as sets in exotic operas, grow only upon the Malabar coast, the island of Ceylon, the Nir Ghirli Mountains, and in Himalayan valleys. In those places untouched by the monsoons and the periodic rains—that is, almost all of Deccan and the northern plains—the sparse vegetation of Islam dominates; coconut palms and banana trees—the pagodas' slender companions—disappear, and the rigid palm and graveyard cypress appear, companions of mosque and minaret.

For two days we have been speeding across the country in trains upon this dense network of railways. All day long the landscape is without variation. The vast tawny plains (red earth and the chattering of crows are the visual and auditory notes of these districts), where rice and millet flourish in the rainy season, are thoroughly parched during the long months of drought. The frail Palmyra palms rise against the blue sky like parodies of palm trees. Vultures and kites hover in the dazzling infinity. On the bright-red horizon herds of gazelle streak past, shadowlike. The tracks are lined by great candelabra cacti, colored red on one side by the dust raised by the wind of the steppe. Each tree is crowned by a contemplative vulture that barely deigns to stretch its winding neck or extend one of its great macabre wings as the train rumbles past. Herds of buffalo and zebu stir, turning their indolent heads, and phalanxes of crows caw on their humped backs and venture into their mouths to peck at the horseflies and flies. Occasionally we plunge into forests of enormous trees with knotted, contorted trunks, but here as everywhere else everything is brown and parched; the branches covered with dry leaves like our oaks in December lend an odd wintry touch to this landscape baking underneath the merciless summer sky. Fair green patches stand out against the dead forest— myriad tiny parrots resembling living leaves or bundles of blue and emerald green embers, families of peacocks perched on the high branches. You emerge from the dead forest and once again see the endless steppe with its ghostly cacti and vultures. We devour distance, time passes, but the countryside is unchanging.

It is the sad time of day, when the traveler wonders why he left fair Italy to undertake this infernal journey. I look away from the bleak scenery. We are in the dining car, where we linger after coffee to prolong the illusion of traveling within a bit of Europe, an illusion generated by the decor, the mirrors, the dinnerware, the food, and the sauces in bottles bearing English labels. These exceedingly spacious cars with double sloping roofs are very comfortable and cooled by three fans; but the mechanism is broken and the *punkah,* a giant fan suspended from the ceiling at the end of the car, is being used instead. An Indian servant seated at the end of the carriage activates it by pulling a cord. English officials, Parsee businessmen, and Afghani dignitaries occupy the tables. Nearby sit two Frenchwomen I chanced upon in Bombay at the Cook agency, where they were having a row; finding them here, once again by chance, prompts reciprocal effusions of joy. In the midst of all these foreigners of all colors, amongst all these horrid tongues—of which pidgin English is the only intelligible one—French, even coming from the retouched lips of these two "wayfaring ladies in exile," sounds as sweet to us as home. The very women who would make you blanch if you were to see them in a European street, with all their paint, dyed hair, ornaments, and feathers—these same women, here in the heart of holy India, add a dissonant but picturesque something to the surroundings. Madame Angot, whom I dreamt about in Golconda, really does live again in these fearless great-great-granddaughters of hers. Back in Bombay they began regaling us with their exploits and misadventures. Young, one of them very young, both Parisian—that is, from Marseilles or Bordeaux—and born into and devoted to their art; as a "duet" they roamed the *café-chantants* from Tunisia to Egypt. At Port Said an impresario signed them on for the East African colonies all the way to Zanzibar. From Zanzibar they fled with two English officers returning to Bombay. Alone once again, they tried their fortunes in Calcutta. Disappointed, they are now making their way toward Shimla, in Kashmir, to sing in a music hall about to open there.

Though frayed by the climate and hardships, worn out by too many stops in too many starving garrisons, that unique French grace remains present in their lively conversation, in a gesture that unites a smile and a cigarette, in the flirtatious manner with which they cross their legs. I watch and admire these two banished songbirds who are carrying their intrepid smiles and gay wares to the ends of the earth.

"DELHI, Agra: le royaume du grand Mogol! Le grand Mogol, Madame, qui avait un penchant pour les jolies Parisiennes."

"Peut-on le voir, ce monsieur-là?"

"He died three hundred years ago."

"Hélas! Nous arrivons toujours trop tard."

We extricate ourselves from the multicolored throng at the huge Indian station. Outside, the most picturesque means of transportation await us: the *jinrickshas,* those light carriages made of lacquered bamboo placed on the newest bicycle wheels, drawn at breakneck speed by bellowing Indians; baroque carriages overloaded with ornaments, bows, ribbons, and bells, drawn by a pair of zebus. Standing neatly ordered to one side, there are also elephants for hire, each of them bearing a sign in several languages indicating the route. You climb aboard one of these giants by means of a kind of gangplank and sit on top with seven others in a small ogee-shaped castle. Both the caparison and the animal are shabby, though they must surely have seen splendid days at some maharaja's palace a hundred years ago. Today the skin on the elephant's immense carcass is wrinkled like the bark of some century-old elm; and the worn, fringed saddlecloth of faded gold does not make him look any younger, nor does the white-blue-red makeup in brightly colored circles around his eyes and upon his trunk.

"Les pauvres oreilles! On dirait des feuilles rongées par des chenilles!"

She's right. The huge ears, black-striped and constantly in motion, are worn through by years of misfortune, the cuts in the huge lobes making them look like moth-eaten leaves. Yet his tiny eyes gleam with intelligence, good nature coupled with cunning, gentleness with resentment.

The *cornac*, a young boy, is seated Buddha-style on the powerful neck and guides the huge mass with an *ankus*, a small curved cane with a hook, which when pressed upon the silent forehead elicits a muted sound of acquiescence. No curses, no abuse of the kind found upon our Western streets. The mass moves forward as confidently as a machine, and the sound of the creature's footfalls is like the rhythmic throbbing of a great motor. We proceed along wide, ultramodern roads, with electric lighting, streetcars, and automobiles; we penetrate tortuous narrow streets lined with tall wooden buildings painted and fretworked like so many samples of confectionery art, with all the colors of candy, surmounted by miradors and tiny loggias; endless covered arcades line and span the streets, connecting one mysterious house to the next.

Our mount places us on a level with the second floor and, cruising between the open verandas, the eye is treated to the most intimate and diverse scenes: a mother consoling a crying child; the office of Parsee merchants, in which five scribes wearing oilcloth miters are seated behind the latest typewriters; a neat and clean Hindu dwelling with white walls bare except for the incarnations of Buddha; a Moslem's house with sumptuous carpets, in which a lean, bespectacled old man wearing a huge turban is on his knees, beating his contrite breast; a native school in which twenty urchins with lively eyes and gleaming white teeth hang out the window as we pass (the teacher is absent), lavishing obscene gestures and insults upon us; and many courtesans, low-caste *bayadères,* recognizable as such by their uncovered faces, their clothing and jewelry, established in the most gaudily embellished houses—strange houses with huge verandas so broadly open as to seriously trouble a visitor's modesty. The elephant, which has met a fellow pachyderm coming from the opposite direction, stops to wait for the other to back into the next courtyard, and we stop very close to the two smiling courtesans. The one with a strange outsized square comb rearranges her smooth pitch-black hair, done into two dusky satin bandages; the other, who is almost hanging out of the veranda, holds a small mirror in her left hand while carefully dyeing her arched eyebrows with her right. Everyone in the town—men, women, children—has splendid, overly large eyes, and the constant use of kohl prescribed by their religion renders these eyes interminable and unreal and confers on these faces the look of an unmindful idol.

"Vois-tu, ma chère, quelle ruse ont-elles à se farder? Elles maquillent seulement la paupière supérieure."

For a few seconds the Westerners and Orientals stare at each other intensely, then the elephant moves on and the vignette is no more.

I BARELY notice the transition from the living city to the city of the dead. Finally there are no more houses inhabited by humans; those populated by monkeys have begun. No more multicolored facades and floral verandas, but buildings as hollow as skulls, surviving walls that enfold emptiness, or the staircases, the sumptuous entrance halls, in marble and granite, of palaces that have ceased to exist: all the wood has been devoured by the steppe. Upon every baluster, every cornice, appear the long tails and sneering faces of quadrumanes. The ruins extend into infinity; the entire steppe, as far as the eye can see and beyond, is the vast cemetery of a city destroyed and rebuilt ten times over in the space of four thousand years. I ask myself by what fatal, mysterious law a city must evolve like all living things, and shoots appear here and there on its decrepit stump, as upon a plant that refuses to die. There is probably no other part of the world where such varied architectural treasures await the archaeologist's spade. In Rome, Greece, and Egypt, all those places sacred to our past, the ghost of civilization is resurrected solely in order that through exhumation, restoration, and study it be brought closer to us. Here, in this desert of rubbish, the reigning chaos of neglect and oblivion is such that the researcher must have the giddy sensation of being hurled five hundred, a thousand, thirty thousand years back into the abyss of time: from the final Islamic splendor of the Great Moghul to the dark Brahmanism of the imposing early Jain and Pali structures, in the dim night of the Vedic origins.

I doubt, however, that archaeologists suffer from poetic vertigo. In this solitude one frequently encounters Russian, German, and English scholars, fair-haired and bespectacled figures, priestly figures who look with scowling indignation upon our profane high spirits. We are at Aladdin's Gate, an immense structure resembling some enormous defunct mosque. Seen from a distance, the size and architectural purity of the mass would suffice to establish it as a model of the Indo-Moorish style; closer by, one discovers that it is wrought like a cabinet engraved by a goldsmith: the entire Koran, with all the most delicate motifs of golden-age Islamic art, decorates the graceful structure, which rises over thirty meters high. The empty space is filled by the bluest Indian sky, and our elephant, motionless in a shaded area, appearing almost minute among these huge ruins, completes that harmonious beauty. Does the very learned—and very impolite—Englishman who is at work in a nearby shed, taking measurements and directing three native scribes busy making drawings and calculations for some government restoration or other, feel this harmony? I have more faith in the enthusiasm and good taste of these French harlots. The more talkative of the two uses adorable images.

"Je l'ai toujours rêvé, ce tableau-là quand j'étais fillette, sur un coussin de ma tante Véronique. Et voilà qu'il y a vraiment une chose comme ça."

Then, drawing her boon companion up to the great carved building and tracing the intricacy of the sculpture with a voluptuous gesture:

"Il faut rappeler cette broderie-ci, pour une robe d'intérieur."

We stroll through the unending ruins. A soulless vegetation, all tin, leather, and tow, a vegetation that has never been alive, alongside the dead stone. Up in the cypresses, in the banyans, gnarled and contorted as by a dry spasm, between the blood-red steppe and the cobalt sky, the masters of the place, parrots, peacocks, and apes, contribute a gay note. How much more beautiful a squat Jain capital with four elephant heads of Ganesa, the God of Wisdom, becomes when all of a sudden a peacock springs upon it, flooding it with a cascade of sapphires and emeralds. How the white marble tracery, representing all the motifs of Islam, comes to life when overlaid by the green of numerous dwarf parrots, the common garrulous parakeets, who play trapeze in the sacred openwork. Endless lines of confabulating monkeys turn their heads as one as we pass by, follow us for a long while, staring at us with desolate, melancholy eyes.

From time to time we come upon a Yogi, a saint who has chosen one of these ruins as his refuge. India abounds in these odd figures. They are not legendary fakirs, nor do they perform miracles, having taken on the color of the stones and dead tree trunks. Completely naked beneath the sun, which frizzles their hair and whose dazzling rays fall upon their upturned faces besmirched with ashes and clay, they sit in the Nirvanic position, more indifferent and unfeeling than the thousand-year-old idols. Custom encourages these sects: each Yogi has a bowl close to hand, which the people fill each day, in their piety. We put questions to one of them as we offer him fruit and a coin. He does not respond to our words or bat an eyelash before our outstretched hands; he lets us go without turning his head, already lost in the divine, in the salvation of desiring no more, already freed from eternal rebirth, healed for eternity of the flesh and the soul. To us these figures seem the most wretched dregs of humanity, yet they are perhaps among all men the only ones to be envied, the only creatures who need recognize no earthly power. "What can you do, O tyrant, what can you do to me, I who am perfectly content amidst the rigors of the Himalayas and the fiery heat of Deccan? You may strike me, O tyrant, you may rend me asunder, burn me, have me killed, but, O tyrant, you cannot harm me."

We walk into the hermitage.

Suddenly, among so many dead things, among so many nameless ruins, we behold something quite alive and well known, in color and line so fresh it could have been built yesterday: the Qutb Minar. I was put off by photographs and prints, even by a certain antipathy. In fact it is the most graceful object a despot's boredom has ever hurled at the sky. An isolated tower three hundred feet high built by a sultan and given to his daughter, who was stricken with melancholy, as one presents a jewel. It is truly a jewel that strikes you from afar with its dazzling height. Close by one gasps before its exquisite workmanship.

The minar looks like an interminable fascine of interminable palms bound at five ascending heights, so that the whole of the slender trunk is pleated like a silken skirt; the salmon-colored stone, inlaid with white marble ornamentation, resembles gleaming fine silk. A work on a scale and carried out with a painstaking execution inconceivable in our times, only possible in ages gone by, when an entire people was the single blind instrument of a despot's whims. Perhaps all these legendary sultans who spent treasures upon the realization of their dreams in great alabaster and marble buildings were in spirit the kinsmen of Ludwig of Bavaria. For the eyes of a beautiful woman they would raze their cities and construct new ones, like Maharaja Sawai Jai Singh II, who in 1728 abandoned Amber, his kingdom's ancient capital, to found

Jaipur, the fantastic pink city, built over a period of little more than three years. They built palaces, temples, and gardens, which they sometimes abandoned before they were completed, already tired of the dream the people took too long to realize in stone.

We climb the lofty shaft and stop to rest at the third, at the fourth circular veranda of fretted marble, where we are seemingly suspended in the void, prey to a pleasurable giddiness. From up there the desolation appears even more despairing; it fills the horizon like a sea of lava and slag, suggestive of the fearful irruptions of those Jain, Pali, Afghan, and Mongol hordes that poured down from the Himalayas and heaped ruin after ruin upon the ill-starred plain.

There stands amidst the tombs, not far from the Qutb Minar, an obelisk that contrasts with the light gracefulness and the flesh tones of the Moorish relic, a barbaric iron pillar that, according to the Sanskrit inscription, Raya Dhava raised two thousand years ago to celebrate his victory over the Valhihas tribe with an object that would defy the ages. It is fifteen meters in height, cast in a single piece, the mysterious document of an extinct, almost forgotten civilization, which nonetheless possessed the means for founding a mass of metal that would be no easy task for present-day industry.

Here, too, I find native and European scholars on the job: archaeologists, experts, architects making models and taking measurements. England is readying for a colossal undertaking: breaking into the bone cave these dead cities are immured within, restoring the ruins, and reordering them decorously in the light of day. A worthy undertaking, yet one I doubt will be favorable to the poetry of these memories. I do indeed thank heaven I am able to visit them today in their state of desolate neglect.

It is the torrid hour; it is also mealtime. Our female companions, "qui ont soupé des ruines," remind us that we have brought along provisions. A providential idea, because the only public house in Aladdin's Gate turns the stomach with its stench of a tannery. We buy a pineapple and enormous fresh grapes shipped from the mountains around Kabul in containers made of huge leathery leaves held together by long strips of weeds—those grapes are a thirst-quenching delight and consolation under this fierce sky.

We seek midday refuge, followed by the *boys* and the *cornac*. There is no end of handsome possibilities: a mosque, a Moorish entrance hall, a Pali royal residence, and a Jain temple. We descend into a cellar known to the *boys:* a shady, cool refuge that would be gloomy but for the gleaming white marble. Huge square columns of stacked cubes support the roof, everything is in monolithic blocks, in a style (in my ignorance I doubt its authenticity) that resembles the most ancient Egyptian, Assyrian, Etruscan, or Phoenician structures, at a time when all these newly born architectures had a good deal in common. An uncanny light pours in through a triangular doorway and four triangular windows; standing in the shade with the burning heat of the tropical noon outside, the five triangles look like the openings of huge furnaces. Enclosed within those five glowing frames are legendary images: arid palms in the distance, the bright ogee form of Aladdin's Gate, lacelike fretted marble; nearby, the baluster of a mosque, and our meditative elephant, rigid on his four columnlike legs, as unmoving as his stone brother.

A time for dreaming. Solace and relief in the coolness and penumbra, the indefinable pleasure of sitting next to friends in a circle and sharing the same meal, the slightly sacrilegious delight of having as companions these desecrators, who say and sing the most outrageous things within these sacrosanct premises. A time for dreaming. Reality vanishes. Objects alter, grow larger, become imaginary and magnificent, like the nutshell, the pebble, the wooden shoe touched by the magic wand in the legend. And I forget. Like someone in the midst of a vast hallucination I gaze at the temple ruins, at my friends, our frugal meal, and these two vagabonds whom even a Western student would not dare claim as his own.

I am the emperor Akbar, the mightiest of the Great Moghuls, and this is my palace; this is a banquet served by three hundred slaves to ambassadors of the Serenissima; these are two "Christian women" seized from Barbary Coast corsairs, sold to the negus of Ethiopia, given by the negus to the shah of Persia, and presented to me by my cousin, the shah—virgins about to reach puberty, delivered to my harem, two fair-haired Christian women to add to my seven hundred concubines of every color.

Heaven help us if we were not able to flesh out with our dreams the meager pleasures that reality concedes us.

Agra the Immaculate

Mᴏʀᴇ than Delhi, Agra enables us to relive the fantastic past of the Great Moghuls. If the last of them, Shah Jahan, were to rise inside his mausoleum and take his beloved bride Mumtaz Mahal by the hand, and they were both to walk forth from their sepulture, the Taj Mahal, they would find the city ever in its splendor and their magnificent palaces respected by time and man. United and superimposed structures, their varied profiles soaring to the height of seventy meters and more, they look more like a titanic heap of feudal castles than an enchanted palace. Yet, on the other side, their light grace flowers high up out of sight, toward the river Jumna and the boundless plain. From the city I can see only the foundations of bright red sandstone, the gigantic walls, and the mighty towers, destined for defense and attack. These forts the Moghul emperors built in India were entrenched camps of a power, scale, and magnificence inconceivable in our time; towns established and fortified, where tyrants with the souls of artists, warriors, and ascetics assembled what they could to satisfy the senses and entice the spirit, from the voluptuary zenana to the halls of government and justice, from the baths to the gymnasium to the purification mosques, and to the mausoleums for final rest. It was a regal city suspended over a city of the people who served prostrate, blinded by so much splendor.

We pass on to the fortified rampart, the towers, the heavy gates. One climbs along dark stairways, under medieval arches; one walks through corridors with loopholes and casemates; and everything is built of red sandstone, everything is dark and massive, evoking in its silence the martial city and the din of arms. Where could the voluptuous life of the turbaned poets and the enormous-eyed beauties have taken place? One climbs and climbs into the dark entrails of the thousand-year-old structure, where the only light enters through an occasional slit; the endless city looks lower and lower as one mounts ever higher within the dark labyrinth.

Suddenly, your hand moves automatically to shield your eyes, assailed by the blinding light of a glacier. We have arrived in the realm of immaculate marble, in the tyrants' celestial city. A vast terrace, then the audience hall, white as all the other buildings and containing nothing but the Great Moghul's black marble throne surrounded by a series of arches that give the illusion of a cavern of frozen milk, of geometrical stalactites, where the whiteness is emphasized by touches of blackest onyx. Onyx, gold, silver, turquoise, and porphyry are used with deft lightness, in delicate floral motifs or lines that follow the complex ornamentation of the lacy marble into infinity, in such a way that the overall white effect is not diminished but increased. Everything is of pristine marble, and one sees only the elegance of its fretwork and engraving perfected to the ultimate limits of an inimitable art. The bathrooms with their rectangular tubs, into which you have to descend three or four steps, seem to be waiting in their smooth whiteness for the floods of scented water, the brown and fair flesh, the silvery laughter of the fifteen-year-old sultanas who have been sleeping for centuries in the plain below.

Our path leads through infinite whiteness. Toward the river the mass of the buildings looks straight down on the plain below and is a more intense profusion of carved marble, loggias, miradors, and observatories where beautiful women dreamt about the subjects of the poets of the day, read Persian strophes with twenty rhymes as complex as algebraic formulas, or licentious tales, or else prayed, holding miniature Korans, for the return of one far away.

One walks from hall to hall; and the halls are doorless so that they form vistas from unspoiled dreams, corridors of white lace that extend into infinity. The limpid freshness of these thin marble slabs is astonishing. Worked with quite incredible skill, these slabs resemble huge openwork embroidery stretched from pillar to pillar rather than stone partitions. You hesitate to touch it, marveling at the centuries-old hardness. Time, which crumbles granite and topples obelisks and temples, has little effect upon marble: these miracles of grace seem to have been wrought yesterday. Surely the plunder-hungry invaders who burst in, leveling and destroying everything in their path, stopped short before the white drapes and lowered their scimitars and maces, as though bewitched. I pause for a moment at one of the observatories, where the beauties of times past have brought on this melancholy I feel. The scene that surrounds me represents the life of the Great Moghuls. The zenana, the harem that jealously concealed the rarest flowers of the flesh, then the immense audience hall, the halls of justice where the sultan and his court, in dazzling brocades and jewels, formed a picture against the white marble that dazzled the kneeling people, then the vast courtyards for jousts, for the tiger and elephant fights, an intense, bloody distraction which the tyrants alternated with the songs of minstrels and the dances of the Devadasi in the tall hanging gardens. All around us, the sheer gigantic walls, symbols of unparalleled power; off to one side, contained in a dark circle and truly resembling a pearl enclosed in a casket, the Pearl Mosque, white, translucent, solemn, simple of line. There, at the end of the city, stands the Taj Mahal, gleaming white in its circle of cypresses and palms: the purest example of funerary beauty ever raised by human hope in answer to the despair of death.

TODAY, sailing along the banks of the Jumna and contemplating the great royal house from below, I am barely able to find the loggias and lacy marble verandas where I dreamed yesterday in the long glowing sunset. The buildings of enchanted marble look like delicate ornaments of snow crowning the reddish mass that was there one or two thousand years ago, during the age of the Brahmin origins, at the time of the Jain and Pali kings. When later the Great Moghuls arrived and seized the gigantic stronghold, they superimposed their lofty home upon it, and upon those tawny granite crests caused pure marble to flower against the azure skies.

Today, on the plain, the lords and their beauties sleep in a royal sepulcher more marvelous than the house they inhabited when alive: the Taj Mahal. The Taj Mahal! I approach the miracle of the Orient with my wonted diffidence before everything too insistently exalted by legend. I prepare to be disappointed as I enter the vast park lined with funereal palms and cypresses. The cypresses form a tunnel, Islamic giants whose almost black-bronze trunks and foliage join overhead. Suddenly, behold the wonder unique in all the world! Seldom has reality so surpassed my expectations, seldom has beauty taken such violent hold of me, leaving me speechless and breathless, compelling my admiration and unbounded, reverential awe. Against the background of two colors— the blue of the sky and the dark bronze of the cypresses —rises the most immaculate and largest structure ever conjured by the imaginings of these white-loving sultans, a structure of a simplicity that defies words and aesthetic analysis. Upon the immense base, a lofty cupola; adjoining it, four tall minarets soaring into space; nothing more. It is the classic motif of Islamic India, the motif profaned by all the Western trinkets, desecrated by operetta backdrops, in crochet-work copies and oleographs, yet in the original truly divine. Of white marble, eternal, yet made of the fleeting translucent stuff of clouds; the billowing cumulus clouds drifting past this very instant behind the immaculate cupola, as if to compete in grace and whiteness, creating in the turquoise sky a contrast less luminous and less pristine. The azure of the sky, the white of the clouds and of the marble, the cypresses' bronze, everything is reflected in a large, tranquil pool that repeats the miracle with the terse whiteness of Persian enamel paintings.

We walk forward, almost incredulous, fearing that the spell created by a necromancer must soon vanish like a mirage. It is only now that I am overcome by the size of the mausoleum. The jubilation of colors had made me forget my sense of proportion. I am brought back to reality by the sight of a procession of pilgrims climbing the front steps. They look like a tiny swarm of ants slowly advancing from one archway to the next. We, too, arrive at the dazzling mass. At close range the dazed eye sees what art constrained to absolute simplicity can accomplish in marble, and we see the Taj Mahal for what it really is: a bulky mass and a jewel; the edifice of a Titan and the masterpiece of a Moorish engraver created from sparse Islamic motifs—geometric ornamentations, garlands of holy words, and delicate floral patterns. Here, too, blackest onyx, carved and inlaid in the marble by a technique unknown to us, following every vault, every fret, enhances the opalescent whiteness of the whole, like a line of kohl traced with a thin brush below the eyebrows increases the flashing pearl of a *bayadère*'s eyes.

Upon the gates of silver—silver against marble's whiteness—is displayed the entire Koran, its constituents, as in a puzzle, at once united and discrete.

I enter the mausoleum. I walk toward the two cenotaphs where the devoted pair who wished to conquer death through love have been sleeping for centuries. For as everyone knows the Taj Mahal was built by Shah Jahan, mad with despair at the premature death of his bride, the fair Mahal (smiling to this day from the enamel paintings and Indo-Persian miniatures), who died in the year 1618, not of an insidious disease, as the sentimental legend would have it, but in dutifully giving birth to a seventh son. Words cannot express my feelings for this genuine tale of passionate, tragic conjugal love. It is said that the deranged widower walked on air through the rooms of the palace, lived as if his spouse were still with him, alive—smiling, talking, calling her by name, pointing her out to his children and his dismayed courtiers. His life became a passionate hallucination, an amorous life with a phantom visible only to him, whom he accompanied upon the terraces and in the gardens, and introduced to his courtiers and his sympathetic subjects at banquets and great occasions.

Out of this madness arose this miracle of funerary art. Love did truly vanquish death. The two hundred-year-old mausoleum is unchanged, as if it had been built yesterday. The loving couple slumbers close to one another, in eternity. Under the sublime cupola more luminous than that of any of our cathedrals, in the windowless penumbra, in its own light, maxims from the Koran are intertwined with delicate floral motifs. Maxims I cannot understand, but which surely must repeat to the two lovers the words that the religions of all nations at all times have said about love and death.

Fakirs and Charlatans

INDULGING a more ordinary kind of curiosity, we are giving ourselves a rest after the recent days' overly intense aesthetic experiences. We visit a workshop where they make carpets. The carpets are beautiful, and the way they are made is most interesting indeed. Thirty workers, for the most part half-naked youngsters, are seated at the loom in a long shed where the heat is stifling. And each worker is in charge of a bobbin of yarn, a single color in the highly complex weft. The overseer, seated on a raised platform at the end of the row of looms, has before him a detailed sketch of the work, with numbers corresponding to the various weavers, and these he sings out in the form of different musical notes; and to the number corresponds the gesture of a little worker, who sings the note back, prolonging it to indicate his agreement. The work moves ahead this way in an at once regular and varied singsong, not without a certain musical sweetness. The overseer looks as though he were conducting an orchestra of very delicately differentiated colors: truly the "symphony of colors" the Decadent poets imagined. From it result these inimitable carpets whose quality and origin appear in the workmanship, simultaneously refined and primitive, in the designs and the naive shifts from one hue to another when a bobbin that has run out is replaced by another or when a left hand

139

takes over from a right, or in a delightful softness, as if one were gliding one's fingertips beneath the wing of a swan. Magnificent pieces of work, which, however, I find attractive only in this setting. In order not to buy, I lower the price. And it is accepted. I lower it again. And it is accepted. I select three carpets. Other merchants come forth from their shops as we walk into the native town and tempt us with a thousand useless items: a Buddha, a Trimurti in ivory, an elephant in ebony standing upright on his bent hind legs and upon his curved trunk holding aloft a large silver tray; embossed pieces in bronze, in copper; veils as fine as woven clouds, dyed on the spot before our eyes with all the most delicate hues of flowers and fruits, then entrusted to a pair of youngsters who run with them to make them dry; amulets, necklaces of gems, the solid gold ornaments worn by *bayadères*. Appealing objects, but which I buy without enthusiasm, for some friends in Italy. I wouldn't want them at home. I know what an exile's melancholy, what a bourgeois dissonance they take on beneath our skies, set between a Louis XV secretary and an Empire cabinet in our modest abodes. Every beauty has its proper setting. However, there are two things I would indeed like to take back with me. The dwelling of the Great Moghul, that palace of immaculate lacework up there on its hill of reddish rock, and the Taj Mahal, with its bronze-green cypresses and its cobalt sky. Today I went back by myself to dwell for hours upon that poem of marble and light. . . . With what longing I shall look back upon it!

THE jugglers and fakirs are a disappointment to anyone who comes to India seeking a touch of the unreal, of the supernatural, but they do contribute a picturesque note to the landscape. Today, in front of the Jain temple, I watched a fight between a cobra and a mongoose, the show that the snake charmers propose to every foreign visitor for only three rupees, which is the price of the victim. Two Hindus, who seemingly just stepped out of a travel brochure—naked, a thin strip of cloth about their loins, huge yellow turbans wrapped around their heads, beards divided and twisted into two hooks, and their ears adorned with solid gold rings—sit across from one another, each with a covered basket between his knees. They start a beckoning prelude, a kind of singsong dialogue, eyeing each other defiantly, menacingly, awfully, now one and now the other raising and then quickly lowering the lid of his basket, shifting their glances toward the attentive audience as if consulting it. Then they reach their decision. One of the baskets stirs, the lid lifts, and the erect head of a cobra appears. It issues with sinuous slowness from its prison, coils, subsides lazily upon the carpet, like an inert cable, its skin gray in color, with black diamonds. And now from the other basket the other adversary suddenly springs forth: a feline that resembles our ferret—a tawny brown, slender, swaying, with red snout and eyes, a bushy tail twice the length of its body, a tail swollen with rage into an enormous red bottlebrush. The cobra rises up amidst its coils, shoots up as if released by a spring, its neck distended, its fury expressed in the dilating pattern on its neck, its flattened head shaken by a continual quivering, like a leaf that stirs in the wind. And surrounded by the cries of the youngsters urging them on and by the deafening thunder of music, the two opponents get ready to attack and to defend themselves, with the mongoose racing around the circular coils as around a fortress, and the cobra twisting upon its axis, keeping its enemy constantly in view. The cobra stiffens, then strikes, dartlike. The mongoose springs backward, protected by the ruddy cloud of its enveloping tail. The mongoose returns to the attack. It is driven off. It returns three, four times; for ten, for twenty minutes the adversaries temporize. Then comes the furious onset, a wild confusion of livid coils and tawny fur until all that remains upon the carpet is one large palpitating ball. The mongoose is lost. But no, the coils slacken, two straining pink paws fight their way free, the bottlebrush tail suddenly comes into sight; the rest of the mongoose emerges triumphantly, disentangled from the reptile which, inert, unrolls: the tiny carnivore has devoured its enemy's brain.

"Not worth watching. The cobra is dry."

An Indian student standing near me touches his thumbnail to one of his incisors, indicating to me that the reptile had no more venom. That doesn't surprise me, given these charmers' familiarity with the terrible intercessor of death. But it is a well-known fact that the mongoose faces up to and destroys wild, untampered-with cobras in the jungle, and it is kept in houses as the watchful and indefatigable adversary of every reptile intruder, as we keep cats for mice.

Some bronze-colored schoolboys, some middle-class men wearing starched collars and carrying bejewelled canes join the circle of jugglers for a moment, then stroll off with an air of snobbish commiseration, turning away from this *quite native* scene, too familiar and too mundane to be of interest. I, however, find delight in observing within this tattered and dirt-poor but picturesque reality the figures and the things too often read about in books. I also find the famous "miracle of the mango seedling" of interest, a prestidigitator's game performed with matchless skill. One of the natives has everyone inspect a genuine mango seed, which he holds up between two fingers, then places in a hole in the ground, covers with earth which he carefully pats down. Over the sown seed he then lays a handkerchief graciously supplied by one of us. Now he begins another trick, to distract the audience's attention. He returns at regular intervals to the mango seed, and each time he does the seedling has added two or three new leaves, until by the end of the performance it has taken on the dimensions of a sapling bearing two fruits and some blossoms. A miraculous growth requiring no fewer than fifty different plants substituted one for the other with such skill that I am unable to see how it is done. I recall the fifty progressively larger wigs of a hairdresser who simulated the growth of a flowing head of hair at the court of one of the Louises of France.

Ah, but what consummate simulators these jugglers are! With what refinements of histrionic art, unknown to our prestidigitators, they deceive and distract our attention; with what mimic art they follow the growth of the mango tree, feigning disbelief before the prodigy, anxiousness, disappointment over early indications of failure, fearful amazement at the first bud, finally the joy of triumph.

Suddenly, the two are quarreling and growing increasingly angry at each other. I take this to be a real altercation when it is only the prelude to another game. Each tries to grab away a ragged sack that they have between them until one succeeds in getting the other inside it and tying him up securely there. Then begins the mimicry of cruel joy, the ferocious dancing around the poor prisoner, who squirms and moans. The unsated captor picks up a club and strikes the bundle until he has beaten it flat, beaten it into the ground, beaten it empty. Then the maniac unties the sack and rummages in it. And he begins a monologue of woe, of despairing remorse, until the crowd divides and one beholds the vanished partner reappear, safe and sound, no one knows how or whence. Surprise, reconciliation, fraternal embraces, and abundant tears—real tears—which shine on their dark lips when the two approach the spectators, inviting us in correct English to give generously.

"A wee little present, Milord! For such poor fellows as we!"

Poor fellows they may be, but of a disconcerting talent and skill, capable, under other circumstances, of picking a howsoever faintly inattentive foreigner's pocket ten times over. And of course it isn't they who are going to provide me with that little bit of the supernatural I had been hoping to find in India, that little bit of the incredible, that little bit of the miraculous . . .

THERE is still only one miracle, only one: the Taj Mahal. We leave tomorrow for Jaipur, and today I went back to the wonder I shall take leave of before I have had my fill of it. The wonder that has the fascination not of a work of art but of a natural and eternal beauty like the sea, the sky, like the highest, most immaculate mountain peaks. It had the color of the granular ice on certain glaciers today as I contemplated it for the last time. Then, as evening approached, it changed to pink and azure, to green, to the ardent violet of steel just before it is tempered. And the bronze-green cypresses, the cobalt sky, and the enclosed waters that repeated the miracle—it is all imprinted inside my eyelids, as when one looks at something blindingly bright.

In six months, in a year from now, lost in the streets of our northern cities, in the mists and the slush of a December twilight, perhaps I shall be able to evoke a bit of this light and these colors beneath my half-closed eyelids, and alleviate the grayness within my soul . . .

Taj Mahal, marble poem of love and death, what a longing for you shall mark my future.

Jaipur: The Pink City

Land of the unexpected! After so many cities of marble, dazzling white, here is one entirely pink—Jaipur. The eye, weary of excessive light reflected from white walls, rests on these palaces as on the softness of certain textiles faded by time. Our imagination finally finds the city of the legend that has inhabited our dreams since early childhood. He must have had the soul of a child and of a poet, that Maharaja Sawai Jai Singh II, who quit the ancient capital of Amber in 1728 and ordered the people to build him a new city, a city such as he had beheld in opium dreams, in Persian fables or Vedic legends. An entire people set to work, and the city rose as if by magic: an immense city, with streets two and three kilometers long, as wide and regular as our finest European avenues, laid out, colored in conformance with a single model, in accordance with the ruler's despotic will. Jaipur is a huge city built following the notions of a single person, the way one has a dress, a necklace, a piece of furniture made. Everything is pink, with delicate floral patterns: houses, arches, domes, mosques' minarets, pagodas' spires—all pink.

I gaze from the hotel veranda, dumbfounded, unsettled. We arrived an hour ago after a three days' ride on the train through the heart of a desolate India, exhausted from the dust and heat, depressed by the landscape that grows progressively bleaker, like an infinite plain of rubble enveloped in an atmosphere both unearthly and unbreathable. Everything is dying in the Rajput states: even the agave, the Palmyra palm, the candelabra-shaped cactus, this tenacious vegetation of tow, leather, and zinc.

And it's classic famine they'd have, the mass starvation of former times, sister of cholera and of the plague, the famine that according to the poet "comes to India to inscribe, with bold strokes of blue pencil, the credits and debits upon Nature's ledger," had England not woven over the whole of the subcontinent a dense network of railways, arteries along which grain, more vital than blood, flows from all parts of the world at the speed of an American express train. Grain, grain—an infinity of bulging sacks piled up in colossal pyramids at every station large and small. The eighty-year-old and the six-year-old, the dancer and the pariah, all betake themselves to the dispensary for their daily ration without saying so much as thank you, without ever understanding thanks to whom and why this gift reaches them. Once everyone has received his measure of grain or white flour, he may devote himself to his favorite pastime: dreaming.

Anyone with an *anna,* or half an *anna,* buys thirty roses—roses sold without stems in constantly watered pyramids—and strings them on a silver wire for his daily garland or walks to the Parsee perfumer for half an ounce of gum benzoin (everyone wears perfume and flowers in this country, even coachmen and cowherds), or buys a wafer of pistachio or a grain of opium or a bolus of betel.

City of dreams and lovable people, which possesses the poetry of the superfluous and the science of useless things. Nothing is more useless than this great rose-colored city. I will surely remember Jaipur if some day I am obliged to choose a homeland for my nonchalance. Italian dolce far niente is a whirlwind of fearsome activity by comparison.

From the veranda of the hotel I look at the regular row of palaces that extends into infinity, draped, one might say, in the same white floral-patterned salmon-colored damask. I am restless; I set forth, cross the street, I wish to see them from close on, to touch my hands to these strange walls. Their surface is a kind of plaster that is three centuries old, harder and smoother than enamel. The houses are narrow, stand cheek to jowl like the medieval palaces in Venice, but they are all the same shade of pink, with patterns that vary infinitely. Oh, the delicate motifs that can be obtained from a little bit of white on a pale red background! Motifs that call to mind the printed cottons, what used to be called "Indian" material: minute lozenges, undulating stripes, swirls, eighteenth-century nosegays, garlands of love knots; infinitely varied, the facades nevertheless blend into the overall harmony, and one has the impression that they will yield to the touch like an immense expanse of cloth hung for a gala.

Pink, everything is pink, to satisfy the taste of a king. The throng moving through these streets seems chosen, trained, and dressed for a choreographic backdrop. In no other Indian city, not even in Hyderabad or in Delhi, did I find an East that corresponded so exactly to the clichés. No streetcar tracks, no automobiles, no Europeans wearing pith helmets and leather boots, but elephants for hire with numerals on their caparisons, nuptial elephants decked in red and gold, painted in the brightest and most varied colors, like Nuremberg toys; camels, drome-daries that go running past, their necks extended, recalling the humorous shapes of certain plucked chickens; little white mules with pink eyes and demure eyelashes; horses—the horses that are missing in southern India—bays, dappled, white: classical Arabian steeds with long flowing manes and tails, ridden by wonderful horsemen you would take for heroes from movies or operetta extras if you didn't sense that they were authentic, *real*—real notwithstanding the gem-encrusted scimitar and the buckler at the saddle bow, the helmet-turban decorated with fluttering plumes, the henna-bleached beard, the eyebrows and eyelashes darkened with kohl. But for whom, for what this theatrical getup of princes out of the *Thousand and One Nights?* Perhaps not so much for the seduction of their docile ladies as worthily to serve the goddess Illusion, the goddess Poetry, the Maya Devi of Indian theogony—she who places betwixt us and "things as they are" the veil of "things as they ought to appear." To be sure, I think with a pang of envy of our so summary Western outfit: solid black or gray suit, stiff collar, soft hat or stovepipe; that's all we are permitted: no bright colors, no feathers or velvet to embellish our ever more restricted masculine charm. Here everyone possesses a princely elegance: princes and cowherds, and not only in the matter of dress. Everyone has the pure beauty of the Aryan type; with them, grace of gesture, gait, and bearing is innate.

In the women beauty and grace reach a perhaps excessive perfection: observing them in the street, their walk, one would say, is something dancelike as with bare, bejewelled feet they tread a straight line, their short steps causing their hips to sway with a provocative rhythm, while their bare arms, encircled by bracelets, are raised to steady strange amphorae of multicolored clay or of copper. They are dressed in brightly colored fabrics and veils, secured by fripperies wound round them from midriff up to the chin; the décolletage, if one can call it that, appears instead at the waist, where bodice and skirt sometimes separate to disclose a good part of the bronzed torso and of the base of the breasts: a décolletage in reverse, which provokes no stirring of the senses, so dignified is their expression and so perfect the beauty of their faces. It is perhaps excessive, perhaps a little monotonous, the beauty of these Rajput women, seemingly all each other's sisters. And all remind one curiously of the Virgin Mary; not the fair-haired Virgin of Western tradition, but the *nigra sed formosa* Virgin of Byzantine mosaics and Coptic enamelwork: the inordinate oval of the face, the mouth formed into a triangular smile, the nose almost too tiny between the very long eyes framed between two bands of impeccably arranged hair that gleam like black satin.

Fairy-tale city. The strangest vehicles go by. Semicircular coaches whose shape recalls that of *bigas,* in which the naked dark-skinned charioteer shouts at and goads the zebus, the Indian oxen—very small, hump-backed, lively, quick-legged, mild-looking, and especially so on account of the long curved horns that sweep back over their humps as though fearful they might cause someone injury. Some other carriages driving by resemble small gilded berlins, with curtains of red brocade. And strange sedan chairs go by, surmounted by a pagoda in which a rich Parsee merchant or a high-caste *bayadère* reclines, or a white-bearded and white-clad dignitary, having about his person nothing dark save his imperious eyes. Each vehicle is preceded and followed by eight or ten servants who advance to the tune of chanted warning, shaking painted palm fronds to left and right or sticks with a long plume of white and black horsehair, actually the tail of a rare species of antelope. There are turbans of every shape and hue: enormous white ones made of rough homespun for the servants and low-caste men; tiny turbans folded and artfully pleated over a form like the little hats worn by our women at home, circular, triangular, or the brim boldly raised on one side, or else falling to hide the cheeks and adorned with gem-studded pins and clasps from which springs a feather, an egret feather or one from a bird of paradise—a hat that would be the envy of our most refined society women.

Fairy-tale city. I walk along beautiful, spacious streets, the broad marble pavements laid in geometric patterns and, from time to time, I brush my hand along the walls of the pink-colored houses, always pink, with delicate white floral designs. What a miracle it is that in a fantastic city like this one the Orient of bygone days has been preserved intact! Here are the court dignitaries, the grooms, the falconers who pass by smiling, holding aloft their hooded falcons—I had read adulatory descriptions of the Jaipur falconers in guidebooks, but I did not believe they existed—and here are falconers as one might have admired them in Tuscany or in Provence on a fine morning in the fourteenth century; and here are the tigers, the Maharaja of Jaipur's famous tigers of which I had so often heard tell in Bombay and Calcutta. They are not tigers, they are panthers—no less beautiful or less formidable. When I am abreast of the Palace of the Winds, suddenly there they are, being led on leashes by a cohort of keepers, some of them creatures that figure in the festival parades. To accustom them to crowds, they are taken for a walk every day after a large meal; there are five in this group—three that are ochre-colored with pitch-black spots, a light-colored one you might call faded, and an entirely black one, a glossy black in which the spots seem moiréd, as in damask. They advance in swift leaps as if they were crossing an expanse of hot metal, the while sniffing good-naturedly in the direction of the naked street urchins who flock about them. When, curious but circumspect, I halt a safe distance away, one of the keepers smiles at me and with a courteous gesture invites me to come closer; he leads the beast up to me; following his example I caress its neck. Its back arches voluptuously, its ears flatten beneath my hand, its eyes close halfway in the bright sunlight; and about its lowered muzzle there is something that reminds me of certain Japanese masks I have seen. Other panthers have gathered around me with their keepers; they rub themselves against my boots, with the blissful purring of large well-fed cats.

CITY of colors. It's as if the people have sought to revenge themselves upon this single color tyrannically imposed upon them by sporting within these pink confines every one of the most vivid hues imaginable: men, women, princes, and beggars, arrayed in rags or silks, percales or velvets; along these streets passes an incessant stream of colors that would be incompatible in our latitudes but blend in this light, in this setting, into a discordant harmony that is a genuine jubilation to the eyes: sulfur yellow, ochre yellow, red, carmine, purple, pale green, willow green, light blue, turquoise.

The dyers' quarter is one of the most unusual things in Jaipur. The dyers ply their trade out of doors, with primitive means and a centuries-old refinement that has no equal in Europe. They move about amidst tubs, vessels, alembics fashioned from huge gourds and coconuts connected by a length of bent bamboo, and grind their seeds and powders in millinery mortars of marble or bronze decorated with the carved elephantine head of Ganesa or the smiling Parvati, "who hath the eyes of a fish." And out of all this they produce linens, tulles which they hang on cords strung in the sunshine, or which they hand over to children whose task is to dry them by running with them. During the running the cloth billows into great kites or else swirls in a serpentine manner about them.

To these people, color is as necessary as light. Women for the most part, women of every caste, crowd around the dye-works. Even the poorest girl always manages to find a copper penny or two to have three yards of faded tulle dipped in the vat, out of which it emerges ten minutes later, dyed the color she is fond of. Upon a solid-color background the artist superimposes the desired design and hue with a marvelous dexterity, now using daubs of silk for the spatterings, now using boxwood rollers, or simply his fingers dipped in dye; from this result marblings, stripes, dappled designs, or areas of the most delicate undulations. So the tulles of the common people, draped with a grace that, as one gazes at these Rajput women, calls to mind the common origin linking them with their faraway Athenian sisters, acquire, through their superimposed transparencies and from the interplay of sunlight and movement, a luminosity that multiplies the effects as it does in a crystal and turns into fairy princesses these creatures who owe their daily subsistence to the government's charity.

EVEN the pigeons are repainted, all of them, like aerial harlequins. As if the natural green of the parrots, the peacocks' blaze of colors, the crows' glistening black did not suffice. So that the pink houses have their white marble dadoes crowned by winged creatures of every color.

There's something else here that I found pleasing and moving. At every crossroads stands a kind of little temple with one column, where charitable passersby leave feed for the birds, which also starve once the last of the vegetation has faded away. Underneath the little pagodalike domes it's a veritable whirlwind of tiny birds: parakeets, thrushes coming and going, trilling their joyous gratitude. They possess the delicate souls of children and Franciscans, these Rajput Hindus, who though besieged by hunger yet feel the need for perfume and flowers, who share a handful of wheat from across the seas with the tiny creatures of Brahma.

ABOUT the maharaja's gardens there is a graveyard melancholy that, however, is not without its charm under these foreign skies. The palms, cypresses, and orange trees are pruned into geometrical shapes between boxwood hedges, Bengal roses, all trimmed after the eighteenth-century French style. Even the pools for the elephants, the ponds for the crocodiles and turtles, have a Louis XV design; and these Western motifs alternate, oddly but not unpleasantly, with Indian lines: spired pavilions, three-bulbed cupolas, little bridges of lacework marble that span almost-dry ponds where the last water lilies and papyruses are wilting. We visit the royal palace—the part of it foreigners have access to—where an anachronism of Eastern and Western elements also holds sway: halls decorated with European damasks, eighteenth-century over-doors depicting Hellenic and bucolic scenes, Robert pendulum clocks, flowers within globes, elaborate tall windows; from these apartments I proceed to corridors with Moorish ogee windows, to verandas of marble wrought to resemble stalactites, to rooms bare of all furnishings but Oriental rugs and cushions within white walls whose only adornment are frescoes representing the incarnations of Brahma. And I mount from one floor to the next of these dream apartments by way of placid electric elevators built in Manchester, while, as a reward, we are awaited in the garden by an elephant put at our disposition by the absent maharaja's Grand Master of Ceremonies. We visit vast gardens, but with sparse vegetation and no shade. Down on the tiered levels of the city, beneath tall orange trees with their drought-withered leaves, gilt cannon alternate with silvered ones, quite as useless and quite as grotesque as the tall, slender, adolescent figures of the soldiers—in their strange uniforms mingling British austerity and Oriental raggedness—drilling in the courtyard below.

Things of an exotic melancholy that words cannot render. And more melancholy than all the rest, the great observatory founded by Maharaja Jai Singh, a lover of the stars, an astronomer whose contribution to science is recognized even by Western societies. In the small inner courtyard, in the middle of a dry basin, an immense soccer court seems to turn on the arched spirals of the marble serpent supporting it. And all around are strange contraptions and constructions of metal and stone in which mysterious formulas are incised; upon them none but squirrels may be seen to meditate today. High above, a wall is crowned by a row of little monkeys, hugging one another, shivering in the dusty evening breeze. The signs of the zodiac alternate with who knows how many pensive little faces and dangling tails.